# YOU WILL ROCK AS A MOM!

## THE EXPERT GUIDE TO FIRST-TIME PREGNANCY AND EVERYTHING NEW MOTHERS NEED TO KNOW

### SIERRA ALEXIS

YOU WILL ROCK BOOKS

**You Will Rock as a Mom!**

*The Expert Guide to First-Time Pregnancy and Everything New Mothers Need to Know*
**Sierra Alexis**

**Table of Contents**

Table of Contents

# CONTENTS

*Introduction*                                                    V

1. I Just Found Out I'm Pregnant, Now What?                         1
2. The First Trimester—Tender, Terrifying, and
   Transformational                                               20
3. The Second Trimester Surprise, Energy (Kinda),
   Emotions (A Lot), and Everything in Between                    39
4. Almost There, Mommy                                            63
5. Birth Day Is Not Just One Day                                  80
6. You're A Mama Now, Gentle Healing, Fierce Love                 99
7. The Baby Bubble, Full of Milk and Magic                       111
8. Finding Yourself While Raising Someone Else                   121

*Conclusion*                                                     129
*Bibliography*                                                   131

# INTRODUCTION

You stare at the little white stick in your hand. The two pink lines are faint, barely visible, but they're there. Your first thought isn't some glow of maternal bliss. Instead, it's, *Oh. My. God. What have I done?*

You sit on the toilet lid like it's a lifeboat in the middle of a choppy ocean, wondering if it's possible to be thrilled and terrified at the same time. You always planned to have kids someday, right? But somehow, "someday" has just morphed into "nine months from now." What do you do now? Call your partner? Google "how to be a mom"? Cry a little? Perhaps all of the above?

Maybe your story looks completely different...

You've been waiting for this moment for years. You've peed on sticks until your bathroom trash looked like a popsicle graveyard. You've whispered hopeful prayers in fertility clinic waiting rooms. You've cried in your car after another negative test. Then, finally, two lines. This time, they're real. They're yours. You feel joy and relief so big it feels unreal. But along with that excitement comes a quieter voice inside: *What if this doesn't last? What if something goes wrong?*

Or maybe you've been here before. You've seen the lines, felt the flutter, picked out names. But, then, you've also known the heartbreak of silence where a heartbeat used to be. Now, those two pink lines are both a beacon of hope and a trigger for grief. You want to believe. You're trying. But you've learned not to get too attached, too soon.

Your story could be completely different. Maybe you're staring at that test thinking, This was not the plan. You were careful. You took precautions. You were living your life, focused on your career. You never wanted to be a mother. Now you're staring at two lines and wondering if there's been some cosmic clerical error. Motherhood? Now? It can't be...

No matter how you got here, planned, unplanned, long awaited, or somewhere in between, you're here. You're pregnant! Congratulations!

Maybe you're excited. Perhaps, you're scared. Probably, you're a bit of both. But here's the deal: Pregnancy is like opening a door to a house you now live in, but you didn't build it, you've never seen the floor plan, and somehow, it's already under renovation.

You'll get advice from every direction: books, strangers, even your cousin's coworker's girlfriend. But most of it sounds like either a biology lecture or a morality tale. What you need is something softer. Something that makes you feel less like a ticking womb and more like, well... you.

Let's get real for a second: 88% of first-time moms say they felt completely unprepared for pregnancy and what comes after childbirth, even if they listened to the advice, took the vitamins, and bought the belly butter (Curran, 2021). That's because no checklist can prepare you for the hormonal chaos, the identity shift, the body weirdness, or the intense swirl of emotions that come with growing a new person.

A good book can hold your hand through it. In *You Will Rock as a Mom!*, we don't shame you for not drinking green smoothies while balancing a crystal on your belly. We don't preach like we're trying to convert you to the Church of Perfect Motherhood. We don't pretend pregnancy is all cute baby kicks, aesthetic bump pics, and zero mental breakdowns in the Target diaper aisle.

This is the book that knows that some days you'll feel like a fertility goddess, and other days like a bloated, cranky gremlin who wants to cry in the shower while slightly peeing yourself. It lets you be real, weepy, hungry, overjoyed, and terrified, sometimes all before lunch.

This book believes moms don't need more pressure; they need more permission to rest, fall apart, feel all the emotions, and most importantly, just be.

This is a space where you're allowed to be messy. You're allowed to not love every minute of being pregnant. You're allowed to say, "I have no idea what I'm doing," and not be judged for it. Through it all, you are still deeply, completely worthy of love, support, grace, and, yes, snacks!

You won't find any toxic positivity here. We're not here to slap a pastel, unicorn-pictured Band-Aid over your anxiety and call it "empowerment." But we'll sit with you in the hard moments. We'll laugh with you, cry with you, even swear a little if we need to. Because pregnancy isn't just a biological event. It's an identity earthquake.

You aren't just growing a baby. You're growing into a whole new version of yourself.

This isn't a medical manual. Yes, you'll find accurate facts and tips, but they come dressed in soft pants, holding a cup of tea and a box of chocolates. Whether you're crying in your car, scrolling forums at 2 a.m., or silently panicking about what's happening to your nipples (yes, we will go there), this book is your companion, not your instructor.

So, if you're overwhelmed, underprepared, and wondering if you're the only one secretly Googling "Is it normal to feel like an alien is hijacking my body?" you've found your people.

Welcome to the tribe! We don't wait until you feel strong to believe in you. We believe in you right now, exactly as you are: nauseous, unsure, scared as hell, but excited.

Because here's the truth: You're not alone. You're not doing it wrong. And no matter how unready you feel, you're exactly where you're meant to be.

**Bonus**

Before we officially begin our journey together, I wanted to give you something special.

Pregnancy is one of the most exciting (and let's be real, sometimes overwhelming) adventures you'll ever take. From the moment you see those two little lines, questions, emotions, and milestones begin to pile up fast.

To help you feel confident, organized, and emotionally supported along the way, I've created a complimentary guided journal you can download instantly. Think of it as your personal space to capture every flutter, craving, and milestone, so you never forget the magic of this season.

Inside this printable journal, you'll find trackers, prompts, and keepsake pages designed to make your pregnancy feel a little less chaotic and a lot more memorable.

**Inside this guide, you'll discover:**

- **Weekly Symptom & Mood Trackers** to capture how you're feeling and what your body is going through.
- **Trimester Goal Sheets** to help you set intentions and celebrate milestones.
- **Reflection Prompts** for journaling your hopes, dreams, and sweet notes to your baby.
- **Baby-Size Chart** so you can follow along as your little one grows from poppy seed to watermelon.
- **Keepsake Pages** to create a memory book you'll treasure forever.

Simply **scan the QR code below** to unlock your free copy of:

You Will Rock As a Mom!: A Guided Journey Through Every Trimester, and start documenting your journey today.

Let's begin!

# 1

# I JUST FOUND OUT I'M PREGNANT, NOW WHAT?

You've had a few days to sit with the big news. You're no longer Googling "Can pregnancy tests lie?" every three hours. The shock is starting to wear off, or, at least, you're starting to get used to the idea, and now comes a new kind of weird. You feel different.

Not just emotionally, although there's that, too (it's normal to cry during dog food commercials). The physical signs of pregnancy may already be there. Your body, which used to be predictable, is now a foreign country. One where your boobs have suddenly declared themselves a no-hug zone. Seriously, brush against a doorframe, and it feels like you've been tased.

Then there's the bloating. One minute you're fine, the next, you're Googling whether it's normal to look six months pregnant after one slice of toast. Welcome to early pregnancy, where digestion slows to a crawl and gas builds up like a pressure cooker.

You might be nauseous, anything from feeling gently seasick to praying to the porcelain god all day long. You might wake up starving and then gag at the thought of food. You might crave pickles, or hate pickles, or want to cry because your partner ate the last pickle. It's all part of this incredible journey where your body starts acting out the script before your brain has caught up.

What's even more confusing is that most of this is happening in silence. You don't look pregnant yet. You might not have told anyone yet. You might be walking around like everything is normal: at work, the grocery store, or on Zoom calls, where nobody knows you're secretly trying not to barf.

This is the beginning. Not the beginning of perfection or of knowing what the heck you're doing. Just the beginning of becoming a mother. One sore boob, one dry cracker, and one quiet breath at a time.

### The Emotional Whirlwind Begins

Let's talk feelings. Because, boy, oh boy, there are a lot of them.

You might feel joyful, grateful, and in awe of the miracle unfolding inside you. You might also feel completely unhinged, swinging from "this is beautiful" to "everything is terrible" in the time it takes to drop your phone behind the couch.

You're not crazy; you're pregnant. If you thought normal monthly PMS was bad, you're in for a ride. Pregnancy can feel like PMS on steroids. Hormones are throwing a party in your bloodstream without asking for permission. One minute you're laughing at memes, the next you're sobbing because someone on a baking show got eliminated. Your partner could blink wrong, and you'll want to pick a fight with them. Or cry. Or both, at the same time.

Then there's the quiet fear brewing under it all. *What if something goes wrong? What if I'm not cut out for this? What if I screw it all up?*

Those are normal thoughts. Uncomfortable, yes, but common.

This is the part where it all begins to unfold, one hormone fueled cry-laugh at a time.

*Pregnancy Anxiety Is Real (And Normal)*

There's something you need to hear, especially in these early weeks when the line between excitement and dread feels paper-thin: You're not negative, ungrateful, or "manifesting bad vibes." You're just pregnant, and pregnancy anxiety is very real.

Anxiety is common in the beginning, when you can't feel your baby move yet and don't have a bump as "proof" of the changes in your body. All you have is a handful of symptoms, a hormone cocktail shaking you like a snow globe, and a brain that has suddenly decided that Googling "5 weeks pregnant no symptoms is it over?" at 2:13 a.m. is a rational plan.

If this anxiety wasn't already enough to deal with, there's the panic. A slight cramp, a little bit of spotting on your panty liner or toilet paper, feeling nauseous all day, and not feeling nauseous all day can make you want to rush to your nearest hospital.

This is the part of pregnancy people don't talk about enough. The part where you're viewing every sensation like you're decoding secret messages from your uterus. You keep checking, wondering, waiting for something that will reassure you it's okay.

If this sounds familiar, you're not alone. You're protecting something precious. That fear you feel is fierce, primal, and instinctive love showing up early. You're already mothering.

I remember searching things like "implantation cramping or miscarriage," "brown spotting 6 weeks normal," "does nausea come and go?" or "how do you know if you're still pregnant?" I was desperate for someone to tell me that what I felt wasn't a bad sign.

Every little thing made me spiral. I was so scared to be hopeful, like it would jinx something.

### *Managing the 2 a.m. Spiral*

The first trimester is full of unknowns, and your brain hates unknowns. It wants data, clarity, and certainty. So you scroll, search, and compare.

But here's the problem: The internet is a giant buffet of everyone's worst-case scenarios, organized by algorithm. It doesn't filter for context. It doesn't know your body. It just knows what makes you keep clicking, and most of the time, that's fear.

Here are a few strategies that might help calm the chaos:

- **Set a "search curfew."** No Googling symptoms after 9 p.m. You're tired. The fear is louder at night. Nothing good comes from a midnight deep dive into Reddit forums.
- **Stick to one or two trusted apps or sources.** Over information can easily lead to overload. Choose one or two trusted apps, and come back to this book whenever you're unsure. Many websites thrive on drama to keep you coming back for more clicks.
- **Use your searches as a signal, not a solution.** If you find yourself Googling the same things repeatedly, pause, breathe, and ask yourself, *What do I need right now? Is it reassurance, control, or comfort?* Give yourself that directly, instead of hunting for it online.

### Grounding Tools for Anxious Moments

You don't have to white knuckle your way through early pregnancy anxiety. There are ways to ground yourself in the moment when it all feels like too much:

- **Breathing exercise:** Inhale for four counts, hold for four, and exhale for six. Repeat this until you feel calmer. Longer exhales tell your nervous system it's safe, which in turn lowers your heart rate.
- **EFT tapping:** This simple technique involves tapping key meridian points (like your eyebrow or collarbone) while speaking calming phrases like, "Even though I'm scared, I trust my body."
- **Journaling:** When your brain starts spinning, grab a notebook and write about your fears, hopes, and questions. There's something powerful about getting the thoughts out of your head and onto paper, where they can't swirl as loudly.

**Your Googling Tells a Story**

Changing the way you're looking at your search history can make a big difference. Sure, you can see it as a sign of your anxiety, or you can see it as your identity as a mother coming to life. Here are a few examples of common searches:

- **Common search:** Nausea remedies
- **What it means:** You're already taking care of yourself
- **Common search:** When to tell work about pregnancy
- **What it means:** You're thinking ahead
- **Common search:** Birth plan template
- **What it means:** You're preparing for the day you'll meet your baby
- **Common search:** Pelvic floor exercises
- **What it means:** You're preparing your body for what's coming

All of this, the worry, questions, and curiosity, is a sign of deep love. You're not just "getting through" the early weeks. You're already parenting, one brave, vulnerable moment at a time.

*When to Tell Others Your Big News*

There's a moment in early pregnancy that feels almost as big as seeing those two lines: deciding whom to tell, when to tell, and how to tell them.

You've probably heard of the so-called "12-week rule." This is the idea that you're supposed to keep your pregnancy a secret until the risk of miscarriage drops in the second trimester. For some, that boundary can feel comforting, like a safe window to wait in before going public.

But here's the truth: The 12-week rule isn't a law. It's not a medical requirement. For many people, it doesn't make sense emotionally.

You're allowed to share your news whenever you feel ready. That might be at 6 weeks, when your body already feels like it's been hit by a hormonal freight train. Or at 10 weeks, when you want someone to know what you're going through. Or, yes, at 12 weeks, or beyond, when you feel safer. All of it is okay. There's no gold star for secrecy, and no curse for honesty.

The only time when the 12-week rule could be seen as a "law" is when telling your employer: Many companies' policies require expecting employees to inform the human resources department at the start of the second trimester. But this could be different depending on the type of work you do and the support you may need, so it's best to check.

### Sharing Is Support, Not a Spoiler

Sometimes we wait because we're scared of jinxing things. Or, worse, what if something goes wrong, and then people know?

But here's the flip side: If something does happen, you might want support. You might not want to navigate the grief in silence. Telling someone can be a way of building a soft landing. It doesn't mean you're expecting the worst. It means you're letting someone into your world, hopes, and reality.

Choose what feels right for you, not what society suggests you should do.

I told my sister at six weeks. I figured, if something went wrong, I would need to cry on her shoulder. And if all went well, I would want her to be part of my joy!

**Three Creative (And Low-Key) Ways to Share the News**

If you're feeling ready to tell someone, whether it's your partner, a friend, your mom, or your whole social media feed, here are a few gentle, joyful ways to spill the beans:

- **Tiny socks on the dashboard:** Leave a pair of teeny-tiny baby socks in the car where your partner will find them. When they ask, smile and say, "We're going to need a much smaller pair of shoes around here."
- **The surprise box:** Fill a little box with subtle baby clues, such as prenatal vitamins, a pacifier, or even your positive test. Wrap it up and hand it over with zero explanation. Watch the confusion melt into joy.
- **Pet announcement:** If you have a dog or cat, pop a sign on them that says, "Guard duty starts [insert due date]." Bonus points for taking a photo and texting it to family members without giving any context or clues. See who is first to figure it out.

There is no need for anything elaborate or "Pinterest-perfect" (unless that's your jam). Simple can be very sweet. Let it match your mood.

**But What if They React Weirdly?**

Let's be honest: Not everyone is great at responding to big news. Some people will cry with joy. Others will go straight into unsolicited advice mode by saying something like, "You know you can't have coffee anymore, right?" A few might even give you nothing but an awkward blink and a "Huh?"

It's okay to feel weird about their weirdness. Here's how to protect your peace:

- **Set boundaries early.** Respond to unwanted advice by saying something like, "Thanks! We're not taking advice now, but I appreciate your support."
- **Have a go-to response for awkward comments.** Try a polite smile and a quick subject change: "Haha, pregnancy is wild. Anyway, how was your weekend?"
- **Give grace, then move on.** Not everyone knows how to respond to vulnerability. That's not a reflection on you or your news. It's just their stuff showing up.

**In Case You Need to Hear It Again**

- Telling early doesn't "curse" anything.
- Telling later doesn't make you secretive.
- You can celebrate, fear, protect, or shout this news in whatever way feels right.

This is your pregnancy. You get to write the rules.

## What's Happening to Your Body?

You might've expected a positive pregnancy test to come with immediate maternal instincts and glowing skin. Instead, what you've got is a body that feels like it's short-circuiting. One minute you're starving, the next you're nauseous. Your boobs feel like they've been replaced with hot bricks. You'll feel cramps and pulls over your abdomen that you immediately believe are bad.

Take a breath. In most cases, what you're experiencing is 100% normal, even when it feels completely bonkers.

Here's a list of the most common early pregnancy symptoms. You might have some of them. You might have all of them. Or, if you're lucky, you might have none of them (Holland, 2024):

- **Extreme fatigue:** You'll feel like you've been hit by a tranquilizer dart before 10 a.m. Your body is working overtime building an entire organ (hello, placenta), so if you feel like a sleepy sloth, you're exactly where you're supposed to be.
- **Breast tenderness:** Your boobs might suddenly be so sensitive that it feels borderline illegal to wear a bra.
- **Mild cramping:** That dull, annoying "Ugh, is my period coming?" feeling is just your uterus expanding, thickening, and auditioning for its new role as Baby's First Apartment.
- **Bloating:** You might feel like someone inflated you with a bike pump. Blame progesterone for slowing down your digestion.
- **Nausea:** For some, it starts as a whisper. For others, it crashes in like a freight train hauling spoiled broccoli. Despite its name, "morning" sickness can strike at any time (or last the entire day).

- **Smell sensitivity:** Suddenly, your partner's deodorant, your neighbor's barbecue, or even your shampoo might become unbearable. Your nose is now operating at bloodhound levels.
- **Darkening areolas:** Your nipples will look dark, sometimes even purple. This is your body's way of prepping for nursing.
- **Frequent peeing:** You'll feel like your bladder has shrunk to the size of a thimble, and your new hobby is locating bathrooms in unfamiliar places. Hormones and increased blood flow to your pelvic area are to blame. So, yes, peeing 14 times before lunch is a thing.

In short, it's like being hungover, jet-lagged, and hit by a hormone hurricane... all while trying to act normal.

### The Hormone Storm

Now, let's talk about the hormones. Right now, your body is being flooded with a tidal wave of pregnancy hormones, mainly (Jennifer Kelly Geddes, 2022):

- **HCG (human chorionic gonadotropin):** This is the one that turns a stick pink and keeps your body from shedding its uterine lining (having your period). It's also the culprit behind nausea and emotional whiplash.
- **Progesterone:** It helps support early pregnancy, but it can make you feel puffy like a human marshmallow.
- **Estrogen:** This hormone helps your body start prepping for baby, especially your blood flow, mood, and yes, those super-sensitive boobs.

Some days, you might feel pregnant. Some days, you won't. There's no right way for it to feel. It's a hormone-powered rollercoaster, and you're doing an amazing job just staying in the seat.

**Quick Pregnancy Body Truths**

Nod along if you've felt any of these already:

- Your boobs can hurt just from existing.
- Bloating makes jeans a hateful invention.
- You're peeing all the time.
- Crying during an insurance commercial is valid.
- You can be both starving and nauseous at the same time.

**Your First Prenatal Visit**

Even though you might want to march into a clinic the second that pink lines show up, most healthcare providers will schedule your first prenatal visit between 8 and 10 weeks pregnant. That's because by then:

- Your pregnancy is easier to confirm using an ultrasound.
- Your baby's heartbeat can usually be seen and heard.
- They can get a better sense of dating and check your overall health.

Waiting several weeks can feel like being stuck in the Twilight Zone. You're pregnant, but no one's officially confirmed it yet. Whether you're nervously counting down the days or already picking out your "I'm chill about this" outfit, it helps to know what to expect.

*What Usually Happens at That First Visit*

- **Vitals:** Expect a check of your blood pressure, weight, and a urine sample. Peeing in cups will become a recurring theme of your prenatal journey. These early vitals help your doctor set a baseline for your health and watch for signs like high blood pressure or protein in your urine.

- **Medical history:** You'll be asked questions about your health, your family's health, past pregnancies or losses, medications, and even past surgeries or health quirks.
- **Blood work:** These tests check your iron levels, blood type, Rh factor, and immunity to illnesses like rubella or chickenpox (*Routine Tests during Pregnancy*, 2021). It's all to make sure both you and your baby start this journey on the healthiest foot possible.
- **Due date calculation:** Your doctor will estimate your due date based on the first day of your last menstrual period, regardless of when conception actually happened.
- **Pelvic exam or pap smear:** This may or may not happen at your first visit. If it is offered, it's to check the health of your cervix and screen for anything that might need attention during pregnancy. Feel free to ask if you're unsure why it's being done.
- **Early ultrasound:** This depends on your doctor. Some do ultrasounds as a standard procedure at all prenatal visits, while others only offer this if there's a specific cause of concern, like spotting or unusual pelvic pain. If you do get one, you might see a tiny flicker of a heartbeat and hear the beautiful phrase, "Everything looks just right." Cue the tears!

It's part science, part paperwork, and all very real. By the end of the visit, the reality of what's happening will sink in, if it hasn't already.

REAL QUESTIONS TO **Bring to Your Appointment (That Actually Matter)**

You don't need to show up with a birth plan or a baby name list, but you can come armed with questions that help you feel informed and supported. Some helpful questions can include:

- What tests or screenings will I need and when?
- What prenatal vitamins do you recommend I take?
- When do I call if I have bleeding, cramping, or other symptoms?
- What's your philosophy on birth plans and interventions?
- What is your policy on inductions, C-sections, and going past due dates?
- Do you work with doulas or midwives? What about hospital policies?
- What support is available for anxiety, depression, or mental health?
- Are there prenatal classes or groups you recommend?
- What's the best way to reach you between visits if I have questions?

You're not being too intense by asking these. You're being intentional.

### Bonding With Your Baby

Right now, your baby is the size of a poppy seed with a tiny heartbeat, and yet... somehow, everything already feels different. You might already feel deeply connected with that poppy seed in your uterus. Or, you might feel like there's no bond at all. Either way, that's completely normal.

The bond will come. Sometimes slowly, sometimes all at once. It doesn't need to be perfect or immediate to be real.

**Small, Simple Ways to Start Connecting**

You don't have to wear a bell around your neck or start playing Mozart through your belly. (Unless you want to, in which case, go full symphony.) Connection can be quiet, tiny, and imperfect:

- **Belly check-ins:** Place a hand on your stomach, even if there's no bump yet. A quiet moment of "Hey, we're doing this together" can start to build a connection.
- **Journaling to baby:** It doesn't have to be deep or poetic. It can be messy, funny, sleepy, or real. Try something like, "Dear Baby, today I felt exhausted and ate string cheese for lunch. I hope you're okay in there." These small notes become tiny time capsules and proof that love can look like snack breaks and survival.
- **Music sharing:** Press play on a favorite song and imagine dancing with your little one. Whether it's a tearjerker or a kitchen bop, music is a powerful emotional connector.
- **Name the weird moments:** When you're suddenly crying over a dropped fork or craving spicy pickles at 10 a.m., take a second to smile and say out loud, "Okay, baby, you're along for this ride, too."

**Why It Matters (Even if It Feels Weird Right Now)**

Studies show that early connection, even imagined or emotional, can support your mental health and your baby's development (Winston & Chicot, 2016). It builds a foundation for how you'll relate to each other over time.

Bonding isn't a switch you flip. It's a process you grow into (and it will get easier as your bump grows). There's no wrong timing. Let this reassure you: Not feeling bonded doesn't mean you're failing. It means you're human, adjusting, and doing your best.

I didn't feel anything for weeks. I kept expecting some wave of love or excitement, but all I felt was tired. It wasn't until I saw the first ultrasound that something clicked. And even then, it came in pieces.

**You, Now: Building a Soft Landing**

So, you've got those two lines, and the initial shock is settling into a million swirling thoughts. Take a deep breath. You've got this. Here's a simple starter checklist to help you take practical steps during Weeks 4–8:

- **Schedule your first OB or midwife appointment.** Getting on their calendar early helps you feel grounded and connected.
- **Start a daily prenatal vitamin.** Look for one with folic acid (prevents neural tube defects), iron (supports your growing blood supply), and DHA (good for the baby's brain development) (*Nutrition during Pregnancy*, 2022).
- **Review your medications and supplements with your doctor.** Common over-the-counter drugs to check on include ibuprofen, acne treatments like retinoids, and allergy pills. Some are safe, others are not, so make sure.
- **Reduce or stop certain substances.** Limit your caffeine intake to about 200 mg per day (roughly 1–2 cups of coffee), or opt for decaf if you want more (*Caffeine*, 2022). As you may already know, alcohol, nicotine, and vaping aren't safe during pregnancy, so it's best to quit any of these habits as soon as possible.
- **Begin gentle self-care.** Hydrate frequently, rest when you can, and focus on easy, nutritious meals that don't require too much energy to prepare. Your body is doing Olympic-level work right now!

**Don't Ring the Alarm Bells Just Yet**

Did you have a glass of wine or pop some ibuprofen before you knew? You're not doomed. It happens. Mention it at your doctor's appointment. Early pregnancy is a big learning curve, and the best thing you can do now is focus on self-care and staying informed.

*The Invisible Wins You Deserve to Celebrate*

Pregnancy can feel like a rollercoaster of big moments: the first ultrasound, hearing the heartbeat, and announcing to family. But what about the quiet victories? The small, invisible wins that don't make for Instagram posts but mean the world when you're living them? Those are the moments you truly deserve to celebrate.

Maybe today, your win was getting out of bed despite the crushing fatigue. Or perhaps you finally asked for help, even if it felt awkward or vulnerable. Maybe you allowed yourself to rest without guilt, shutting down the voice that says you should "just push through."

These wins are powerful. They are the foundation you're building on, day by day. Sometimes, survival itself is success. Sometimes, softening into your body and emotions, instead of fighting them, is the bravest thing you can do.

To help you recognize your invisible wins, try this exercise by completing these sentences:

**My little wins this week:**

- Today, I got out of bed even though I felt tired...
- I asked for help when I needed it for...
- I rested without feeling guilty after...
- I listened to my body and took a break when...
- I spoke kindly to myself when...

Filling in these blanks can turn your attention to what's working, even when the bigger picture feels overwhelming. It's a gentle reminder that progress isn't always flashy. It's often quiet and unseen.

Remember, your journey is uniquely yours. Celebrate the invisible wins. They're the true markers of strength and love.

*Truths No One Tells You (But You Deserve to Know)*

Being newly pregnant can feel like entering a secret club, and half the time, you're not sure if your body is celebrating or rebelling. You Google things you never imagined ("Why do I smell metal?"), second-guess your every move, and ride a carousel of emotions.

So, here's your permission slip to stop pretending you have it all figured out. Below are real-deal truths that many pregnant women wish someone had told them sooner. We've already answered some in this chapter, but you can use this as a quick reference when you're too tired to search for detailed answers:

- **Question:** Why do I feel like I've been hit by a bus?
- **Answer:** Because you're building a placenta. It's the Olympics of organ creation. Your system is flooded with hormones, your metabolism is shifting, and your blood volume is starting to increase. So, if your biggest win today is brushing your teeth, happily accept your gold medal.
- **Question:** Why do my sweatpants feel like leggings overnight?
- **Answer:** Bloating is a beast, and it shows up before any baby bump does. Thanks to progesterone, your digestive system slows down. That plus increased fluid retention can make you puffier than a Thanksgiving parade float. It's normal, it's annoying, and yes, it gets better. Until then,

stretchy pants, small meals, and lots of water are your new best friends.

- **Question:** Why do my nipples hurt when I sneeze?
- **Answer:** Breast tenderness, especially in early pregnancy, can feel like your chest is staging a protest. Your milk ducts are growing, blood flow is increasing, and your hormones are playing DJ with your pain sensors.
- **Question:** What if I don't feel excited but just scared?
- **Answer:** Pregnancy is a huge, life-altering shift, and fear is part of the deal. Joy and anxiety can coexist. Give yourself grace. You're allowed to feel how you feel, without guilt or explanation.
- **Question:** I feel disconnected from the baby. Am I failing already?
- **Answer:** Nope, not even close. Bonding is a process, not a pop quiz you missed the study guide for. Disconnection now doesn't mean anything about your future as a parent.
- **Question:** Is it weird to already be annoyed at everyone?
- **Answer:** No, it's not weird. It's hormonal (and sometimes even justified). Your body and brain are recalibrating under a tidal wave of estrogen and progesterone. Your tolerance for nonsense has temporarily reduced to zero. Whether it's your partner's chewing, your coworker's perfume, or the way the world feels louder, this irritability is common.
- **Question:** Can I still eat sushi? What about coffee?
- **Answer:** Good news: You don't have to say goodbye to all your favorites. Certain sushi (like cooked rolls or vegetarian options) is still on the table. Coffee is allowed, just keep it to about 200 mg of caffeine a day. Always check with your doctor or midwife if you're unsure.
- **Question:** What do I do if I've already done something "wrong"?

- **Answer:** Almost everyone finds out they're pregnant after the fact, and that fact often includes wine, sushi, hot tubs, or a double espresso. One "oops" doesn't undo the incredible work your body is doing. Mention it at your first appointment so your doctor is in the loop. Then let it go.
- **Question:** Can I still be me while being pregnant?
- **Answer:** Yes, a thousand times, yes. Pregnancy isn't the end of your identity. It's an expansion of it. You don't have to trade your sense of humor, passions, or boundaries just because you're growing a human.

Your body's changing faster than your brain can catch up, and in the next chapter, we talk about all the WTF things happening under your skin (and in your bra). It's about to get weird and magical, all at the same time. Welcome to the first trimester!

# 2

# THE FIRST TRIMESTER—TENDER, TERRIFYING, AND TRANSFORMATIONAL

Not enough people talk about how long or strange the first trimester feels.

It's only 12 weeks, but it can feel like a hundred days of holding your breath. You're pregnant, but it doesn't quite feel real yet. Most people don't know. You don't look different. You can't feel movement. You're just waiting...

Waiting for the first appointment. Waiting to feel something more certain. Waiting for the moment it sinks in. Waiting to shout your big news from the rooftops. Waiting to feel pregnant.

While you're waiting, your body is already in full-blown action mode. Cells are dividing. Organs are forming. Hormones are spiking. You're the blueprint, the builder, and the power source, and somehow, you're still expected to answer emails and act normal in public.

It's the weirdest mix of silence and chaos: Your body has become a waiting room and a construction site at the same time.

Let's talk about the chaos part. Up to 90% of pregnant women experience nausea in the first trimester (Smith et al., 2025). That's right: not 9%, but 90! That's almost everyone. Yet, nobody warns you that throwing up into your handbag outside CVS is normal.

You're suddenly furious at your partner for chewing or breathing too loudly. Coffee smells like roadkill. You cry because you can't get a wasabi-flavored donut at midnight. And somewhere around week seven, you find yourself Googling "Can fatigue make me legally dead?"

This isn't a glow-up. It's a grown-up. Your body is doing something big. Quietly, awkwardly, sometimes hilariously, but it's doing it. Even when you're not sure how.

So, no, you're not imagining it. You're not overreacting. You're just in the first trimester: The only time nausea, crying over sandwiches, and being irrationally mad at your partner's cologne is 100% valid.

**What's Actually Happening?**

You don't have a bump. You don't glow (unless "clammy" counts). But inside, you are a full-blown science experiment.

You might feel exhausted, bloated, moody, or like you're secretly hosting a frat party in your uterus: loud, chaotic, and full of questionable fluids. While you're lying on the couch desperately trying not to break gas, your body is doing something amazing: It's building a tiny person from scratch. Let's break it down.

*Weeks 5–6: And Just Like That… Your Organs Are Making Organs*

At Week 5, your baby is about the size of a sesame seed, but things are happening fast. The neural tube is beginning to form, the start of your baby's brain and spinal cord! The circulatory system is also kicking into gear. A primitive heart is forming and will soon begin to beat, somewhere around 110 beats per minute (Peterson, 2023). That's almost twice the rate of yours! By Week 6, tiny arm and leg buds are sprouting, and the face is starting to take shape, even if it's still more alien emoji than baby photo.

Inside your body, there's a major hormone surge happening. Estrogen, progesterone, and HCG are tripling down on their mission: Grow this baby at all costs. The placenta is under construction, and while it's not fully online yet, your system is already working overtime to build it.

You might also feel light cramping or tightening in your lower belly. This is due to your uterus stretching and thickening its lining to support the pregnancy. It might feel like a "period-lite" version of your normal cramps, just enough to make you question what's going on every few hours.

All of this is happening before your pants stop fitting. You don't need a bump to feel pregnant. Emotional whiplash, nausea, and the overwhelming need for naps are all valid signs of the life growing inside you. Your experience matters, even if no one else can see it yet.

Realizing I was growing a brain inside my body helped me cope with my brain that had gone missing. No wonder I couldn't find my keys.

### The Surprising Perils of Gardening (And Other Unexpected Hazards)

Your body is suddenly very sensitive. Smells can become completely intolerable. Cleaning sprays might seem suspicious, even if you've used them for years. And it's best to leave painting the house to your partner or hired help while you stay far away from the fumes.

Here's what to keep an eye on in early pregnancy:

- **Cleaning products:** Avoid heavy-duty chemical cleaners, especially those with strong fragrances or bleach. Choose natural, fragrance-free options instead. A simple mix of vinegar and baking soda can work surprisingly well. It's also best to stop dyeing your hair in the first trimester.
- **Pesticides and solvents:** Skip them completely. If your home projects involve painting, refinishing furniture, or using strong adhesives, let someone else take over.
- **Gardening:** Be cautious when handling soil. It can carry toxoplasmosis, a parasite found in cat litter (Deganich et al., 2022). Always wear gloves, and wash your hands thoroughly afterward, even if you're just repotting a houseplant.
- **Foods to double-check:** Some processed meats (like deli meats), raw fish, and soft cheeses can carry bacteria if not heated or pasteurized. Check the guidelines, ask your doctor, or skip altogether.

I cried when I found out I couldn't clean with my favorite lavender scented spray anymore it really took a toll on me. Then I cried because I was crying.

### Weeks 7–8: Welcome to the Chaos

Your baby has officially doubled in size (again), and your body is shifting gears like it's late for something. By Week 7, your baby is about the size of a blueberry (Gates, 2025). The arm and leg buds are starting to bend at the elbows and knees, like tiny gummy limbs in motion. Deeper inside, the digestive and respiratory systems are beginning to take shape.

In Week 8, the transformation keeps rolling: Fingers, toes, eyelids, and even a visible upper lip are now part of the mix. The tail that was once part of the embryo is gone, and by the end of the week, your baby graduates to official fetus status. This is a big week for such a little tenant.

Your symptoms may also go into an extra gear, but not everything in early pregnancy is as obvious as nausea. Some symptoms sneak in under the radar and make you question everything, such as (Gates, 2025):

- **Metal mouth:** You might notice an odd, metallic taste, like you've been chewing on nickels. As unpleasant as it can be, it's nothing to worry about. Just rinse your mouth out with mouthwash.
- **Extra saliva:** Some women experience increased drooling, especially in the mornings or during nausea.
- **Round ligament pain:** As your uterus grows, you might feel sharp or pulling pains in your lower belly, especially when you move quickly or change positions.
- **Discharge changes:** Increased vaginal discharge that's thin, milky, and odorless is a normal part of the hormonal shift. If it changes color or smell, definitely talk to your doctor.
- **Headaches:** Hormone surges, plus low blood sugar or dehydration, can lead to tension headaches. Small, frequent snacks and lots of water can help.
- **Skin surprises:** Some moms-to-be see their teenage acne return with a vengeance. Others develop super-sensitive skin. This is all due to the hormones that have taken over control of your body.

I called my OB because I kept getting these sudden, shooting pains down my leg. I was sure something was wrong. She said it was totally normal. I'm still horrified and wanted to move into the spare room.

**Fitness and Movement: Stay Strong, but Stay Smart**

Exercise during pregnancy can be a great way to support your body, boost your mood, ease discomfort, and prepare you for the beautiful hell that is vaginal birth. The sooner you start being active, the more you'll thank yourself when you're waddling toward the end of the nine months.

The rules of exercising change a little when you're growing a tiny person (Pillai, 2025):

- **What's safe:** Low-impact activities like walking, swimming, and prenatal yoga are excellent choices. Gentle stretching, deep breathing, and pelvic floor strengthening (hello, Kegels!) can keep you feeling strong without overdoing it.
- **What to avoid:** It's best to skip contact sports, hot yoga, or anything high-impact that involves jumping or jarring movements. Also, avoid exercises that require lying flat on your back for long periods, especially once you hit Week 12.
- **Hydration matters:** Drink water before, during, and after any movement, even a light walk. Staying hydrated helps regulate body temperature and prevents dizziness.
- **Watch for overheating:** Steer clear of saunas, steam rooms, or workouts in high heat. If you're sweating buckets and feeling faint, it's time to stop and cool down.

### The Not-to-Do Gym List

Here's a quick guide to what's best to avoid right now:

Not Recommended

• Avoid basketball, soccer, martial arts, or anything with a high risk of falls or being hit in the abdomen.

Heavy Lifting That Strains the Core

• Skip max-effort lifts, Olympic-style weightlifting, or holding your breath while lifting (Valsalva maneuver).

Deep Twists or Aggressive Core Work

• Avoid deep abdominal crunches, sit-ups, or twisting poses that compress the belly.

Jumping, Hopping, or Sudden Direction Changes

• Reduces risk of falls and unnecessary joint strain (pregnancy hormones loosen ligaments).

Holding Your Breath During Exercise

• Always breathe steadily, oxygen flow is crucial for you and your baby.

**Safer Alternatives**

- Contact sports

- Walking

- Hot yoga or hot Pilates

- Prenatal yoga (cool room)

- High-impact aerobics

- Swimming or water aerobics

- Lying flat on your back (after Week 12)

- Side-lying or seated stretches

- Core crunches and planks

- Pelvic floor and deep breathing

Always listen to your body. If fatigue hits you, give your body the rest it needs. Remember, pregnancy is a marathon, definitely not a sprint. Some days, you might feel like you're auditioning for a role in a fitness movie, while other days, you'll barely have the energy to make it to the toilet. And that's okay.

### Weeks 9–10: Digestive Drama and Decision Fatigue

By Week 9, your baby is about the size of a grape and already working on its next growth spurt (Donaldson-Evans, 2024). By Week 10, it's grown to the size of a kumquat, with fingers and toes fully separated, and joints that can now bend (Marple, 2025). Tiny teeth buds and internal organs are taking shape. While you can't feel it yet, your baby has started making small, wiggling movements.

Internally, most of the major organ systems are formed and beginning to function. It's wild to think about: Your baby has kidneys and a liver doing their jobs before you've even figured out which leggings are tolerable this week.

Meanwhile, your body is dealing with the drama. Thanks to slowed digestion, you might notice more constipation, bloating, or gas. You might also start seeing veins appear more prominently on your chest or breasts, a normal sign that your blood volume is ramping up. Some moms experience occasional dizziness or lingering headaches, often tied to hormone shifts or blood-sugar dips.

Nausea might finally begin to ease, or it might reach its peak. Or, perhaps, it might be completely gone one day, only for you to hurl at the thought of food the next. Just go with the flow. This is also often the start of weird food cravings. Yes, my new mom friend, it's normal to want tuna and peanut butter together on a slice of toast.

I cried once because I wanted spaghetti with maple syrup, and there was no syrup. Then I got mad at myself because I knew how ridiculous and nasty it sounded!

Emotionally, these weeks can bring a wave of decision fatigue. This is usually when your doctor may bring up prenatal screening options like Non-Invasive Prenatal Testing (NIPT) or the Nuchal Translucency (NT scan) (*First Trimester Screening...*, 2022). These are totally optional and designed to screen for chromosomal conditions or potential anomalies. Here's a simple snapshot of what you might be offered:

**Test, When It's Done, What It Screens For, How It's Done,** NIPT

Around Week 10

Common chromosomal conditions such as Down syndrome (Trisomy 21), Trisomy 18, Trisomy 13, and sex chromosomes. Offers early, highly accurate info from a blood draw; can reveal the baby's sex.

Weeks 11–13

Measures fluid at the back of the baby's neck to assess risk for chromosomal conditions

Done by ultrasound and is sometimes paired with bloodwork for added clarity

You might feel relieved by the extra information, or anxious about what it could mean. Both reactions are completely valid. Choosing to test (or not to test) is personal. Discuss this with your doctor, as their insights and advice may help you decide.

*Weeks 11–12: The Invisible Work You Deserve Credit For*

You've been climbing uphill in fog, nauseous, tired, and overwhelmed, and now, whether or not it feels like it, you've made it to the ridge. Weeks 11 and 12 mark the final stretch of the first trimester. This is a milestone, even if it doesn't look like one.

By Week 12, your baby is fully formed, fingers, toes, heartbeat, organs, all present and accounted for (Morrison, 2017). From here on out, the focus shifts to rapid growth and refinement. Baby is now about the size of a lime and capable of subtle movements, although you won't feel them just yet.

The placenta is stepping up, taking over hormone production. That means the wild fluctuations of the past several weeks could start to level out. For many, this brings relief. For others, the chaos takes a different form. Either way, what you've done is no small feat: You built the foundation for a human being.

You might expect to feel better now, and maybe you do. Or maybe your nausea is lingering, your pants still don't fit, and you're staring at your partner like they've never chewed louder in their life.

Symptoms can shift, but that doesn't mean they vanish. Some women get a small burst of energy. Others feel even more tired, mentally and emotionally. And that's okay.

**First Trimester Debrief Checklist**

- *Did I get through it?* Yes, you did.
- *Did I learn something about myself?* Probably more than you expected.

- *Do I still feel unprepared?* Probably, but that's completely normal.
- *Is this a new beginning?* Absolutely.

## Your Week 11–12 Manifesto

You're entering the final weeks of the most intense hormone storm of your life. You don't owe anyone polished excitement. What you deserve is space to process and strength to move forward with care.

Here are five gentle permissions for the road ahead:

- You don't need to reply to every baby advice text.
- You don't have to enjoy your body right now.
- You don't need to catch up on any pregnancy to-do lists.
- You're allowed to ask for space, even from people who love you.
- You're doing enough simply by making it to tomorrow.

You've done the invisible work. Now, take a breath. You're not at the end (not even close), but you're not at the beginning anymore, either.

## Wait, Is This Normal? The First Trimester's Plot Twists

Pregnancy is supposed to come with a manual, right? One that explains why your nipples feel electric, why you just cried over a paper towel that fell on the floor, or why the sight of chicken suddenly feels like betrayal? Unfortunately, that manual doesn't exist. What does exist is this section, which will help you through some unexpected moments.

This is your safe space for every "Is this normal?" moment. The weird stuff no one warns you about in cute announcement videos.

You're not alone in wondering, Googling, or second-guessing every bodily sensation. Let's take a deep breath and sort through what's common, what's worth calling your doctor about, and what's just your body doing some wild, incredible, and very confusing work.

### Miscarriage Fears vs. Actual Red Flags

There's a specific kind of anxiety that shows up between Weeks 6 and 12: the fear that something might silently go wrong. Maybe you've had a previous loss. Perhaps, you've heard one too many stories. Or maybe you're just overwhelmed by how much is changing inside you.

If you've ever found yourself doing any of the following, then congratulations! You're wildly, deeply normal:

- Checking your underwear every time you go to the bathroom
- Retaking pregnancy tests for reassurance
- Obsessively Googling "Is nausea supposed to disappear?"

There's no shame in fearing the worst. That fear is not a failure of optimism but a sign that you care deeply.

I actually panicked when my nausea disappeared for 48 hours. Turns out, it was just two good days. Then it came back with a vengeance.

### When to Call Your Doctor

No one ever wants to sit on a knife's edge, fearing the worst will happen. You also don't want to disregard anything that might be serious. So, how do you know when you should rush to the hospital or take a few deep breaths to calm down? Here's a list of symptoms that might be a red flag (Nordqvist, 2023):

**Call Your Doctor If...**

Mild cramping that feels like period pain

Cramping that's severe or one-sided, and doesn't go away

Light spotting (pink or brown), especially after sex or an internal exam

Bright-red bleeding or heavy flow like a period

Nausea and occasional vomiting

You can't keep food or liquids down for more than 24 hours

Mood swings that make you cry during comedies

Sudden intense anxiety, depression, or intrusive thoughts

Fatigue that makes 3 p.m. feel like midnight

Fainting and dizziness that doesn't go away

No symptoms at all (yep, this happens!)

You had symptoms, and they all suddenly disappeared with other concerning signs (like bleeding or pain)

Breast soreness, bloating, and smell sensitivity

Pain or burning sensations while peeing and fever

Throughout this book, we might say "doctor," but this could be anyone providing your healthcare, such as an OB-GYN (the specialist doctor who delivers babies), midwife, nurse practitioner, or other provider. If you have questions, that's exactly whom you should reach out to.

## If You've Experienced a Loss, or Do in the Future

This part matters deeply. Most early miscarriages are caused by chromosomal issues that were entirely outside your control. It's most likely not caused by eating a deli sandwich, taking a hot shower, having sex, stress, traveling, or standing too long in Target.

Let this sink in: Up to one in four pregnancies end in miscarriage (Simelela, 2024). Most women go on to have healthy, full-term pregnancies afterward. If this has been your experience, or ever becomes your experience, please remember that you aren't broken. You're still a mother. Your grief matters. And you're not alone.

### Food Cravings: When Comfort Comes in Carbs and Chaos

The moment it begins, it's unmistakable. A sudden, undeniable craving for cheese, citrus, or a very specific brand of freezer waffles. Welcome to the era of food as a full-on identity crisis. Salty carbs, lemons, and grilled cheese are the holy trinity for many in the first trimester.

It's not just weird cravings that will leave you feeling confused. You might also experience sudden aversions, especially to meat, eggs, or anything green and leafy. It's confusing, personal, and often downright frustrating.

Here's the golden rule right now: Eat what you can stomach. The goal is survival, not perfection. And remember:

- **Food can be emotional.** You might find yourself mourning your usual love of spinach or crying over the wrong brand of crackers.
- **Taste buds have gone rogue.** You might want a banana at 9 a.m. and gag at the smell of one by noon. Right now, your body is a chemistry lab, and your taste buds are the

interns, confused, inconsistent, a little dramatic, and just trying their best.

If you've been beating yourself up about what you're eating (or not eating), stop. You are not failing if:

- You ate crackers for three meals. It still counts.
- You only drank ginger ale for a week. That's hydration and soothing, especially if you're struggling with morning sickness.
- You can't stand your prenatal vitamins right now. That's normal, and it doesn't make you a bad parent.

### Survival-Mode Eating Is Still Eating

Let's reframe food guilt with a few first-trimester affirmations:

- Crackers are a food group now.
- A popsicle for dinner is still nutritious if it stays down.
- This is survival mode, not failure.

Just to be crystal clear: Eating "badly" for a few weeks won't harm your baby. The placenta hasn't even fully taken over yet. You've got time to find balance later. Right now, the priority is getting through the day.

When you feel ready to sneak in a few gentle nutrients, here are some easy, no-pressure ideas:

- **Fiber-friendly snacks:** Apples with nut butter, overnight oats, or chia pudding can help digestion without overwhelming your system.
- **Gentle proteins:** Try eggs, string cheese, hummus, Greek

yogurt, or smoothies with a scoop of nut butter. These are easy wins that likely won't turn your stomach.

- **Hydration helpers:** Lemon water, broth, coconut water, or herbal teas such as ginger and peppermint can keep you hydrated and grounded.

You don't need to be perfect. You need to be cared for. That includes extending care, grace, and nourishment to yourself, one bite (or sip) at a time.

### The You Underneath It All

You're growing a human. That is amazing, but it can also mean that you feel lost, in yourself, your new reality, and your identity. But that's not the case. Sure, you're upgrading your title to that of "mom," but that doesn't mean that you've lost your "you."

### *Building Early Communication With Partners and Support Systems*

You might have moments when someone asks how you're doing and you answer "fine," only to cry in the bathroom five minutes later. Or maybe your partner comes home proudly holding ginger ale, thinking they've fixed everything; meanwhile, you haven't pooped in three days.

This isn't about blame. If you can't predict your moods, how can they? Am I right? They can't know how your brain feels hijacked by hormones, how food smells different now, or how your insides ache with both joy and confusion. So, how do you start bridging that gap?

Start with honesty, even when it feels small. Here are a few conversation starters you can try:

- "I don't need solutions; just someone to hear me right now."

- "Can we make a plan for when I'm feeling off emotionally?"
- "It would help me if you checked in once a day about how I'm doing physically."
- "Let's talk about whom we're telling and when; are you ready?"
- "Here's one thing I need more of, and one thing I'd love less of."

It's okay if the dynamics of your relationship are complex. Whether you're parenting with a boyfriend, girlfriend, spouse, donor, co-parent, surrogate, or solo with a village behind you, flexibility is the magic ingredient. There's no one way to build a family and no perfect script for how to do this together.

Shared rituals help. They don't need to be fancy or spoken, just consistent. A few examples of how your partner can help you include:

- A daily foot rub
- Sending each other calming songs or playlists
- Five minutes of quiet hand-holding, without talking, scrolling, or expecting sex
- Setting up a shared grocery list with a friend or partner
- Letting someone drive you to an appointment
- Creating a meal swap (or snack swap!) with a neighbor
- Accepting help, even if you could technically do it yourself

Support isn't weakness. It's connection. And yes, your partner can become an emotional MVP, even if right now they're floundering. You can teach your partner to step into what I like to call *Emotionally Available King Energy*. That means learning to read a room, holding space instead of offering fixes, and being present and steady instead of perfect. Your partner can read about this in our *You Will Rock as a Dad* book series.

**Single Moms, Listen Up**

If you're going this path solo, by choice or circumstance, please hear this: Being the only adult in the room doesn't mean you have to do it alone. You can build your support pod: a friend who texts every morning, a sibling who runs errands, a doula who truly sees you, or an online group where no one says, "just wait until the baby gets here."

Create a safe support list of three to five people you can call or text when things feel heavy, joyful, or completely ridiculous. Pregnancy is enough. You don't have to be invincible.

*Who's That Body?*

While your baby is growing furiously inside your womb, your body won't feel quite like yours anymore. Your pants don't button. Your bras feel like bear traps. Your face might puff up a little, your skin may go haywire, and yet, no one on the street would guess you're pregnant. It's like living in disguise.

You're allowed to grieve your old body or feel unsure about this new one, even if you're thrilled about the baby. Take a moment to reflect on this: *What feels different in my body, and how do I talk to it with kindness? What can I do to feel grounded again?*

Here are a few suggestions:

- Wear clothes that fit your body right now, not clothes that shame it into silence.
- Swap out your routine for something gentle and luxurious, maybe a nontoxic lotion or a good body oil.

- Greet yourself in the mirror with playful neutrality: "Hi, hormone warrior," or, if you're feeling playful, "Hello, again, marshmallow boobs."

Comfort creates confidence. This is not the season for tight jeans. Pack them at the back of your closet. You can take them out again once you're not a human incubator anymore.

In the beginning I never fell in love with my pregnancy body like those Instagram posts suggest you should. But when I stopped fighting it I started to love it.

You've done 12 weeks of invisible, relentless work. Now, it's time to make space mentally, physically, and emotionally for what's next. In Chapter 3, we'll talk about bump days, nesting urges, body changes, and the magic (and mess) of the second trimester.

3

# THE SECOND TRIMESTER SURPRISE, ENERGY (KINDA), EMOTIONS (A LOT), AND EVERYTHING IN BETWEEN

Welcome to the second trimester: the magical middle child of pregnancy. This is the part everyone swears is the best. You've supposedly graduated from the nausea olympics, your jeans have surrendered to stretchy panels, and you might even get a compliment or two about your glow (which could be sweat and strategic highlighter, but you thank them anyway).

Yes, this is often dubbed the "honeymoon phase." There are definite perks: Food starts tasting good again, your energy makes a surprise comeback, and your bump looks more like a pregnant goddess and less like a weird lunch situation. But here's the truth nobody puts on the cute trimester chart: Just like the rest of pregnancy, the second trimester can be downright weird.

One minute, you're organizing baby clothes by color and crying happy tears over tiny socks; the next, you're sobbing because you dropped an apple and are now questioning your ability to parent a human. Your emotions are having a dance party, your bladder is making life choices for you, and the Google rabbit holes continue getting deeper. Cue the searches: "Is it normal to feel kind of sad at

21 weeks?" "Can my baby hear my voice yet?" "Do raccoons carry baby-safe diseases?" Don't worry; we've all been there.

The second trimester is the part of pregnancy when things start to feel real. You might hear the heartbeat. You'll see your baby waving like a little astronaut during the anatomy scan. Your maternity pants become less of a fashion choice and more of a survival strategy. And your brain is quietly shifting from *What is happening to me?* to *Oh, wow, I'm going to be somebody's mom!*

This chapter is your no-filter guide to the middle stretch: the good, the odd, the miraculous, and the moments you'll tell stories about years from now while your kid eats crackers off the floor. Let's dive in.

**What's Actually Happening**

All right, you've survived (or barely survived) the first trimester, and now you're smack dab in the middle of the pregnancy rollercoaster. This is when things start to get real. Your body is changing in ways you might barely recognize, and your baby is growing faster than your weekend to-do list.

*Weeks 13–17: The Transition Zone*

Welcome to the "Is that a bump or am I just bloated?" phase. Between weeks 13 and 17, your uterus is making its grand entrance, slowly rising out of your pelvis and giving your belly its first real chance to pop. This is when people might finally stop wondering if you're just carrying a little extra weight.

You might start feeling those infamous baby flutters: The tiny pops and bubbles that feel suspiciously like gas but are way cuter. Some babies are chill and slow-moving at first; others throw tiny dance parties. Feeling the baby's kicks this early during pregnancy is usually more common during second or third pregnancies. If you're a first-time mom, you may have to wait until closer to the 20-week mark (or even a bit later) to feel your growing ninja.

If you ever worry about movement later on, tracking kicks becomes a real thing: You count every time you feel some movement. Once you get to 10 counts, you can relax, knowing your baby is just fine. Because pregnancy can make your brain feel foggy, it can be helpful to make a note on your phone or keep a notepad close to make tracking easier.

Physically, you might notice energy shifting. The mythical energy boost may show up. Cravings are back, and can often be confusing. Who knew that salad and Doritos drenched in ketchup are a winning combo? Round ligament pain might become stronger with sharp tugs as your body adjusts. Nasal congestion could also show up. Just use a saline spray to loosen it, or ask your doctor for pregnancy-safe meds.

This is also the "waiting for the big moments" phase: first baby shopping, anatomy scan, gender reveals, and those tender first talks to your bump (sometimes even first dreams about your little one).

Let's talk about sex drive: Some moms feel a boost and can't wait for their partners to come home, while others want to ghost their partners entirely. Both are completely normal and the luck of the draw. Feeling more frisky is due to increased blood flow to your vagina, but this can also cause more sensitivity down there. Just take it as it comes.

Some days, I felt like a glowing goddess and couldn't get enough of my husband, and the next day, I wanted to nap while cuddling with a bag of chips. I just stopped making any plans in advance.

.   .   .

*WEEKS 18–22: Surprise! Your Baby Has Eyelashes*

Your baby's eyebrows are coming in (and probably already better groomed than yours). You might experience some of pregnancy's weirder symptoms: vivid dreams that feel like soap operas, little skin tags popping up, nosebleeds that appear like uninvited guests, and the infamous pregnancy brain where you forget why you walked into a room... twice.

Common discomforts make their grand entrance, as well: Hello, back pain, hemorrhoids (yeah, we're saying it), swelling, and constipation. A surprisingly effective and pregnancy-safe way of treating constipation is to add a teaspoon of olive oil to your juice. It helps to add oily moisture for things to "slide out" more easily.

You may see a dark line appearing on your belly. It's called linea nigra, and as much as you might not like your new look, it's completely normal and typically disappears within a few weeks of giving birth (O'Connor, 2022). You might also start to experience Braxton Hicks contractions. These are practice contractions, preparing your body for the real deal. Even though the intensity of these practice contractions is nowhere close to what you'll experience when baby is coming, it causes many pregnant women (especially first-time moms) to rush to the hospital. But don't worry, we've got you covered. In Chapter 5, we'll help you spot when to call your doctor.

Around week 20, the halfway mark of pregnancy, you'll likely be scheduled for a detailed ultrasound known as the anatomy scan (Jabaz & Abed, 2023). This is a big moment. It's not just about checking for the baby's sex (though that's often part of it, so if you want to keep it a surprise until the birth, do tell your OB-GYN); it's a head-to-toe medical assessment that gives doctors a close look at your baby's developing body.

During this scan, the technician or doctor will carefully examine the brain, heart (yes, all four chambers are there!), spine, kidneys, stomach, bladder, limbs, and even count tiny fingers and toes. They're looking for signs that everything is growing as it should and for any anomalies that might need follow-up.

For many moms-to-be, this scan is deeply emotional. Seeing the intricate chambers of the heart flickering on the screen, or watching a tiny hand wave or foot kick, can suddenly make everything feel so real, like meeting your baby for the first time in high definition. There's often a swirl of feelings: awe, relief, love, and sometimes nerves. But mostly, it's a quiet moment of proof that inside you, a whole little person is growing, organ by organ.

**To Reveal, or Not to Reveal**

Ah, the age-old question: Should you find out the baby's gender before birth, or wait for that delivery-room surprise? The answer is up to you, and there's no right or wrong way to go about it.

Some parents-to-be love the idea of knowing early. It helps with planning the nursery, buying those tiny clothes in just the "right" color palette (hello, blush pinks and sage greens), or even narrowing down baby name lists without needing a spreadsheet. Others love the mystery, suspense, and picturing that once-in-a-lifetime delivery moment when someone shouts, "It's a...!"

If you do decide to find out, there are different ways to reveal the gender. For some, it's a low-key text to family or a simple "We're having a boy!" caption on social media. For others, it's a full-blown event with cupcakes, confetti cannons, or a mysterious smoke bomb. (Spoiler: The smoke rarely seems to stay contained.)

While these celebrations can be fun and memorable, they don't always go as planned. Like the couple whose balloon box refused to open, leading to a ten-minute wrestling match with duct tape in front of 50 guests. Or the dad-to-be who swung a bat at a color-filled baseball, missed, and got smacked in the face. And who could forget the backyard party where the "It's a girl!" fireworks set a small bushfire? Remember that if you want one of these gender reveals, and it doesn't go according to plan, your guests will probably enjoy it much more than if it all goes perfectly.

Whether you reveal in private, go all out with a party, or wait until the delivery room for your plot-twist ending, it's a deeply personal decision. Go with what feels right for you. And maybe, keep a fire extinguisher handy. Just in case.

I had this friend who had a gender reveal and tried to pop a giant balloon filled with confetti, but it floated away before they could hit it. So, basically, her gender was first revealed to a random passing airplane. She ended up having a boy!

### Weeks 23–27: Baby Showers, Back Pain, and Big Feelings

Welcome to the tail end of the second trimester, often referred to as the "golden weeks" of pregnancy. You might feel a little more energetic, a little more "glowy," and a lot more emotionally invested in the tiny person growing inside you. Or you might still be riding the emotional rollercoaster, tearing up over baby socks one minute and wondering if you'll ever sleep through the night again the next. Both are normal.

This is a great time to deepen your emotional bond with your baby. Talk to your bump, sing to it, read out loud (even if it's just your grocery list), or play music you love. Babies can start responding to sounds during this stretch, and your voice becomes a familiar, comforting melody. You might create sweet little rituals with your partner, like nightly belly rubs, talking through name ideas, or imagining your baby's first giggle. Journaling your hopes, worries, and wild dreams for the future can be very grounding.

You might also think more seriously about what's next: birth plans, maternity leave, parenting styles, child care, and how exactly one swaddles a newborn without creating a baby burrito disaster. These thoughts can bring excitement and anxiety in equal measure, and it's okay if you don't have it all figured out. No one does.

Identity shifts tend to bubble up here, too. Maybe you're starting to feel like a mom, even if the title still feels surreal. You might notice changes in how you see your body, admiration for its strength, frustration with discomfort, or awe at how much it's doing. It's okay to feel proud and uncomfortable all at once. You're becoming someone new, inside and out.

This is also prime time for baby shower planning. Whether you're going full Pinterest-board with games and themed cupcakes or keeping it low-key with just a few friends and some good food, the shower often brings a sweet dose of celebration, and maybe a few tearful moments when you realize just how many people are cheering you on.

Meanwhile, baby name debates may start heating up. You might discover that your partner hates your lifelong favorite name or that your mother-in-law has very strong opinions. Just remember: The final call is for you and your partner to make together. If you don't like the family name that half of your relatives already have, you can break this tradition.

The nesting instinct can also show up as you get closer to the third trimester. Some people find themselves organizing drawers at 2 a.m. or impulse-buying drawer organizers they didn't need. Others feel no urge to fold baby onesies by color, and that's okay, too. There's no one right way to prepare for your baby's arrival.

Then comes the magic moment: outside kicks. You'll place a hand on your belly (or someone else will) and feel that flutter, thump, or tiny alien-looking bump beneath the skin. It's surreal. It's intimate. It's the kind of moment that makes everything pause, just for a second, and makes it all feel so real.

As you're nearing the end of your second trimester, I encourage you to take a few minutes to reflect. What have you learned about yourself since you saw that positive pregnancy test? How has your world shifted? What are you most looking forward to? What scares you the most about childbirth and becoming a mother? As you do this, remember, you're growing in every sense of the word.

**Setting Belly Boundaries**

As your bump becomes more prominent, you might notice something odd: People suddenly think your body is community property. Whether it's a sweet older woman at the farmer's market or a curious coworker, unsolicited belly rubs are common. Some moms don't mind; others find it deeply uncomfortable. Either way, you get to decide what's okay.

If you're not up for the surprise touch, here are a few gentle but effective ways to handle it:

- **The kind redirect:** Smile and say, "I know it's tempting, but I'm not big on belly touching." Most people will get the hint without hurt feelings.
- **The humor route:** Try, "Careful! Baby's charging rent now for belly touches." A little laugh can ease the awkwardness.
- **The firm-but-polite:** A simple, "Please ask before touching" is perfectly acceptable, and sometimes necessary.

Don't beat yourself up for freezing if someone catches you off-guard. You're navigating a lot right now, physically, emotionally, and socially. Learning how to assert new boundaries is just part of the wild, wonderful prep work of becoming a parent.

I was in the grocery store comparing cereal boxes when I saw an old friend and they reached out and rubbed my belly like I was a lucky Buddha statue. I was too stunned to speak. Luckily, after a solid minute I got the gut too tell them not to touch me.

## Make Room: Home Prep and Baby Space

There's a moment, sometime in the second or third trimester, when it suddenly hits you: A whole new person is moving in. They'll need space, not just in your heart, but in your home. Creating that space can feel exciting, overwhelming, and surprisingly emotional. Whether you're planning a picture-perfect nursery, carving out a cozy corner in a studio apartment, or simply rearranging some drawers, this chapter is all about making room, physically and emotionally, for this new chapter of your life.

### *The Nursery (Or Not): Creating a Space That Works for You*

Let's bust a myth right away: You do not need a fully styled nursery to welcome your baby. If you have the space and it brings you joy to decorate it, by all means, go for it. But if your baby's first home will be a bassinet next to your bed, a portable crib in the living room, or a drawer with a blanket in it (no judgment, people have done it!), that's perfectly fine.

Babies don't need much at first: a safe place to sleep, a few essentials, and loving arms. Many parents opt for "rooming in" during the early months, keeping the baby close by for night feeds and bonding. Some don't set up a full nursery until later, once they understand their baby's rhythms.

If you do want to prepare a baby-specific space, keep it simple and functional:

- Start with a safe crib or bassinet and a designated diapering spot (even if it's just a changing pad on a dresser).
- Set up a little night station, including water for you, burp cloths, fresh diapers, wipes, nipple cream, snacks, and your phone charger. You will thank yourself for this during those midnight feeds.
- Add a soft lamp; a chair you love; and something that makes you smile, such as a favorite quote, a plant, or a photo of your support team.

Whatever space you create, make sure it works for your life, not someone else's Pinterest board.

**Nighttime Truths No One Tells You**

- You might fall in love with a crib that your baby won't sleep in until month five. That's okay. It makes a great laundry holder in the meantime.
- You'll become a master of stealth as you lower a sleeping baby into a bassinet like you're handling an ancient artifact on a pressure sensor.
- You may swear you'll never co-sleep... until the third night of cluster feeding at 2 a.m. and your arm becomes a mattress.
- You'll try to "sleep when the baby sleeps," but somehow that's always when a package gets delivered, the dog barks, or your brain wants to rehash every life decision since 2003.

- You will Google "normal newborn breathing sounds" at 3 a.m. and fall down a rabbit hole of baby sleep Reddit threads.
- Your partner will snore peacefully beside you while you consider throwing a burp cloth at them. Out of love, mostly (sometimes).
- Nighttime feeds will feel endless, until one night, when your baby sleeps through and you weirdly miss the quiet stillness of those 2 a.m. baby gazes.
- You will become a human pacifier, snack bar, and cuddle dispenser.
- There will be nights when no one sleeps and mornings when you wonder how you're still standing. But somehow, you'll keep going, and that makes you a superhero in soft pajamas.

### The Great Declutter: Making Physical and Emotional Space

It starts innocently enough: one drawer or one shelf. Then, suddenly, you're knee-deep in old mugs, sorting cables from 2012, and wondering why you've kept so many mismatched socks. Welcome to the nesting declutter. It's part cleaning spree and part emotional transformation.

Making space for a baby often means saying goodbye to other things: unused furniture, clothes that don't fit anymore, or remnants of a former life that no longer feel quite like you. It's more than just organizing. It's preparing your environment to match the new version of yourself that's emerging.

A few gentle tips:

- Do a little at a time. Focus on one area each week.

- If it doesn't support your comfort, your baby's needs, or your peace of mind, it can probably go.
- Don't be afraid to ask for help. Friends or partners can be great sorting buddies (especially when you can't bend over easily anymore).

If you feel like you're not doing enough prep or your space isn't coming together as planned, give yourself some grace. Babies don't measure love by closet organization.

### Inviting Help: Visitors, Boundaries, and Shared Spaces

The baby isn't the only new arrival in your home. Soon, you'll have a parade of eager visitors: friends, grandparents, coworkers, or neighbors. Sure, they might bring muffins, but they often stay just a bit too long. Having people who love you and want to support you is a gift, but it's also okay to protect your space and peace.

Here's the truth: You're allowed to set boundaries. It's one of the most important things you can do to protect your emotional and physical well-being after birth.

Start thinking now about what kind of help and company you want postpartum:

- Do you want people to visit you in the hospital, or wait until you're home?
- Do you want to limit visitors to certain times of the day?
- Are you okay with drop-ins, or do you want people to call or text first?
- What kind of help do you need? This could be someone bringing meals, doing laundry, or holding the baby so you can shower.

Remember: Visitors aren't just coming into your house. They're entering your new family bubble. It's okay to lovingly say, "We'd love to see you in a few weeks once we've found our rhythm." Or, "We're asking everyone to keep visits short so mom and baby can rest."

If you're sharing your home with others after the baby arrives, like a parent coming to help, or a friend staying over, have those conversations now. Who's doing what? Who's helping with meals or laundry? Who's taking the night shift with the baby so you can sleep? Getting it clear up front can prevent resentment later.

Bottom line: You're not being rude or ungrateful when you say no. You're creating space to rest, bond, and recover. That's what good parenting starts with: protecting your energy.

After my baby was born, I loved it when friends and family popped in with meals and snacks. But, somehow, they often brought well-meaning opinions and unwanted advice with them. Eventually, I sent out a text that stated to always let us know before heading to see the baby, so I was able to pick the people that didn't give me headaches around.

**Budget Boot Camp**

Let's be real: Babies are small and cute, but their stuff? Not so much. Between the stroller aisle that looks like a car dealership and the pressure to create a Pinterest-worthy nursery, it's easy to feel like prepping for your baby means draining your savings account. But here's the truth: You don't need everything, and with a bit of planning and budgeting, you can take a lot of the stress out of the process. Let's take it one smart, sensible, no-guilt step at a time.

. . .

*PLANNING Your Finances Without Losing Your Mind (or Your Savings Account)*

You're growing a whole human, and now it feels like you also need to become a part-time accountant. Take a deep breath. Yes, babies come with expenses, but with a little planning and a lot of perspective, you can do this without panic-Googling "Can I cloth diaper with paper towels?" at 2 a.m.

Let's walk through the real numbers, smart strategies, and budget hacks that help you prep for baby without blowing your entire paycheck on tiny shoes they won't even wear.

Here's what you're really looking at with basic baby costs in the US (Longman, 2024):

**Item**

**Average Cost**

Diapers (first year)

$500–$900

Wipes

$150–$300

Formula (if used)

$1,200–$1,500/year

Crib and mattress

$150–$400

Car seat

$100–$300

Stroller

$100–$600

Baby clothes (0–6 months)

$200–$400

Nursing supplies

$100–$300

Miscellaneous gear (e.g., tub, nail clippers, thermometer)

$150–$300

Reality check: You don't need the fanciest stroller with Bluetooth speakers or a bottle warmer that plays lullabies. You need the safe basics, and the rest is optional. In the next chapter, we'll look at gear that most moms consider to be "must-haves" and those that rarely get used.

**Budget Hacks That Help**

- **Buy secondhand.** Babies outgrow everything so fast. Look at local consignment stores, neighborhood swaps, Facebook Marketplace, or Buy Nothing groups. Just check for recalls and safety standards on gear like cribs and car seats.
- **Accept hand-me-downs.** If someone offers you clothes or gear, say yes. You'll thank them when your baby explodes out of a diaper on hour four.
- **Skip the "tiny luxury" trap.** Organic bamboo socks? Adorable. Necessary? Not so much.
- **Rotate and re-use.** A pack of 10 burp cloths is gold. They double as bibs, blankets, changing pads, and emergency spit-up shields.

### SAMPLE MONTHLY PREGNANCY Budget (Just a Guide!)

No one likes the word "budget," especially when you're already juggling hormones, nursery planning, and midnight cravings. But having a simple, realistic budget can bring you peace of mind. You don't need to cut out every latte or track every penny, but you do want to get a sense of what to expect and feel more grounded as the big day gets closer.

This sample monthly pregnancy budget isn't a one-size-fits-all plan. It's a flexible guide to help you think about where your money might go, what's essential, and what can wait. Whether you're super spreadsheet-savvy or just want a nap and a snack, this can help you make choices that support your values, your baby, and your future.

**Category**

**Estimated Cost**

Housing/rent

$____

Groceries

$____

Medical co-pays

$____

Baby savings

$____

Maternity clothes

$____

Baby items

$____

Fun/sanity fund

$____

Even saving just $10 per week from now until delivery adds up. You're not budgeting for perfection, just progress.

If money's tight (and, hey, even if it's not), you're not alone, and there is help. While the help available will depend on your location, here are some of the more popular options for moms in the United States:

- **WIC (Women, Infants, and Children):** WIC provides free healthy food (think fruit, veggies, milk, eggs, and cereal), breastfeeding counseling, infant formula, and nutrition education to pregnant women, new moms, and kids under age five (*WIC: USDA's Special Supplemental Nutrition Program for Women, Infants, and Children*, 2023). Some locations also offer breastfeeding supplies and connections to other community resources.
- **Who qualifies:** You typically qualify if your household income is below the federal poverty level (but many working families still qualify, so don't assume you earn "too much"). You must be pregnant, postpartum (within 6 months), or have a child under age five.
- **How to apply:** Contact your local WIC office (just Google "[your state] WIC" or call your state's health department). You'll need to bring proof of income, ID, and proof of residency. Once approved, you'll get benefits either on a card or in paper vouchers to use at participating grocery stores.

- **Why it helps:** WIC helps ensure you and your baby get the nutrition you need, especially when food prices feel overwhelming. And it's not just about groceries; it's about peace of mind.
- **SNAP (Supplemental Nutrition Assistance Program):** SNAP provides monthly funds on an EBT card (i.e., a debit card) that can be used for groceries, including fresh produce, meat, dairy, and pantry staples (*Supplemental Nutrition Assistance Program (SNAP)*, 2025).
- **Who qualifies:** Eligibility is based on income and household size. Many pregnant women qualify even if they're working. You don't need to be on other benefits to apply, and in some states, applying for SNAP will also screen you for other programs such as Medicaid.
- **How to apply:** Visit https://www.fns.usda.gov/snap/state-directory to find your state's application. You'll need basic income and ID documents. Applications are usually online, and decisions are made within 30 days.
- **Why it helps:** SNAP frees up your income for other baby needs, such as wipes, gas to get to appointments, or saving for maternity leave.
- **Medicaid's Children's Health Insurance Program (CHIP):** Medicaid covers prenatal doctor visits, lab tests, ultrasounds, delivery, postpartum checkups, and often, mental health support. In many states, CHIP (a partner program) covers your baby after birth, including wellness visits, vaccinations, and pediatric care (*Children's Health Insurance Program (CHIP)*, 2022).
- **Who qualifies:** Income eligibility varies by state, but pregnant women often qualify even if they didn't before pregnancy. Some states offer "Presumptive Eligibility," meaning you can get temporary coverage immediately while your full application is processed.

- **How to apply:** Visit https://www.healthcare.gov/medicaid-chip/ or call your state's Medicaid office. You'll need income documentation and proof of pregnancy (often a note from your doctor or clinic).
- **Why it helps:** This coverage can lift a massive financial burden. No more stressing over copays or hospital bills when you're just trying to focus on keeping you and your baby healthy.
- **Local programs:** Many towns offer diapers, baby classes, and support groups. Check with your hospital or community center.

There's nothing weak about needing support. It's strong, smart, and exactly what these programs are for.

### *Baby Shower and Registry: The Smart Mom Strategy*

Creating a baby registry is one of those "I can't believe this is real" moments. Suddenly, you're scrolling through endless lists of swaddles and snot-suckers, trying to guess what your future baby might need and what you'll actually use. But take a breath: You've got this. With a little planning, your registry can be a powerful tool for prepping and a sweet reflection of your growing family.

Most parents-to-be start building their registry around 20 weeks, right after the anatomy scan (and sometimes right after finding out the baby's sex, if you're choosing to find out). That's far enough into pregnancy to feel real, but early enough to give friends and family plenty of time to shop before your shower.

**Top registry platforms moms love:**

- **Amazon:** A universal registry with fast shipping and group gifting options makes it simple and convenient for guests.

- **Babylist:** Lets you add items from any store, including Etsy and local shops, and even non-traditional gifts like a meal train or a diaper fund.
- **Target:** Ideal for in-store shoppers and comes with a generous one-year return policy on registry items.

Most sites offer perks like a completion discount (10–15% off items not purchased) and free welcome boxes of baby goodies.

**Baby Showers on a Budget (And From the Heart)**

You don't need a balloon arch that can be seen from space to have a meaningful, beautiful shower. Some moms opt for:

- **Potluck backyard brunches:** Family and friends contribute food, so there is less stress, less financial burden, and more flavor.
- **Virtual showers:** Great for long-distance loved ones.
- **Book-themed showers:** "Bring a book instead of a card" is adorable and practical.
- **No-frills gatherings:** Pizza, cupcakes, and a "blessing circle" to share wishes and advice. It doesn't get better than that.

The most magical showers are the ones where you feel loved, supported, and celebrated. Remember: These aren't just for the baby, but for the mom you're becoming.

**Common Baby Registry Mistakes to Avoid**

- **Too many newborn outfits:** They outgrow them in 3.4 seconds. Get a few cute outfits, but focus on 0–3 months and up. Work out the seasonal needs of every size set of clothing and send this to your guests, so your baby has

summer clothes that are the correct size when it is
summer.

- **Not enough practical items:** You'll need more wipes than
  onesies, and burp cloths over baby shoes.
- **Ignoring your lifestyle:** If you're a city dweller who
  doesn't go for regular jogs, that jogging stroller might not
  be for you. Don't register for what looks cute. Register for
  what fits.
- **Skipping mom-focused items:** Don't forget nursing bras,
  nipple cream, peri bottles, and snacks. (You're part of the
  equation, too!)
- **No variety of price points:** Some guests want to splurge,
  others need budget buys. Include a few options in both
  categories

### Planning Like a Boss: Maternity Leave, Income, and Work

Let's talk about a topic that's often equal parts exciting and overwhelming: work and maternity leave. Understanding your options
can feel like learning a new language, so here's a cheat sheet:

- **FMLA (Family and Medical Leave Act):** If you've been at
  your job for at least a year, you may qualify for up to 12
  weeks of job-protected, unpaid leave (*Family and Medical
  Leave Act*, n.d.). That means they have to hold your job,
  but they don't have to pay you.
- **Short-term disability insurance:** This sometimes covers a
  portion of your income (typically 50–70%) for 6–8 weeks
  after delivery, depending on your policy and whether you
  had a vaginal birth or a C-section (Guardian Editorial
  Team, 2016). Some employers offer this automatically,
  while others require that you sign up in advance, so
  check now.

- **Unpaid leave or paid time off:** If you're not eligible for FMLA, you might still be able to use paid time off (vacation or sick days) or negotiate a personal unpaid leave with your employer.
- **Company-specific leave policies:** Some employers go above and beyond, offering paid parental leave or return-to-work benefits. It never hurts to ask HR for a copy of your company's maternity policy. You might be pleasantly surprised.

**Questions to Ask HR (Or Yourself!)**

Write these down and take them to your next HR meeting:

- How much maternity leave is available to me? Is it paid or unpaid?
- Am I covered by short-term disability, and how do I file my claim?
- Can I use paid time off, vacation, or sick time toward my leave?
- Do you offer flexible return-to-work options, such as part-time, remote, or phased return?
- What benefits continue during leave, such as health insurance or 401 (k)?
- Is there a parental leave policy separate from disability leave?

**When (And How) to Tell Your Boss**

Most people wait until after the first trimester to share their news, typically around 13–20 weeks, when the risk of miscarriage is lower and you've had a few appointments. But as we've already said, there's no single "right" time. It's about when you feel ready.

Legally, you are not required to tell your employer until you're ready to request leave. However, some companies have very specific policies on this, so it's best to double-check.

Whether you're telling your boss in person or over email, here's a sample you can tweak for your vibe:

**In person or via Zoom:**

Hi [Boss's Name], I wanted to share some exciting personal news. I'm expecting a baby due in [month]! I'm still working through my leave plans, but I wanted to give you plenty of time to prepare. I'm fully committed to supporting the team and ensuring a smooth transition. I'd love to set up a time to talk through ideas when you're ready.

**Email template:**

Subject: Exciting News

Hi [Boss's Name],

I wanted to let you know that I'm expecting a baby, due around [month]! I'm currently learning about my leave options and would love to talk through any planning steps that would be helpful for our team. I'm happy to help make the transition as smooth as possible and will keep you in the loop as I learn more.

At the end of the day, this is more than just paperwork or policy. You're protecting your health, peace of mind, and time to bond with your new baby. You deserve that space, and with a little planning, you can claim it with confidence.

I agonized over telling my boss I was pregnant. I practiced in the mirror like I was giving a TED Talk. But when I finally did, she said, "Congratulations! We'll figure it out." I spent so much time worrying and zero time realizing I deserved that moment of joy.

YOU'VE DECLUTTERED YOUR CLOSET, tamed the baby budget, and maybe even survived your gender reveal without setting anything on fire (win!). But just when you thought you had a grip on things... your body shifts again, your emotions surge, and the finish line suddenly feels too close.

The third trimester isn't just a countdown; it's a transformation. Your belly, mindset, to-do list... all of it ramps up. In the next chapter, we'll guide you week-by-week through the final stretch, help you prep, and remind you (loud and clear) that you're not alone.

Ready or not, Mama. It's go time.

# 4

# ALMOST THERE, MOMMY

"I feel like I'm running out of time to become the perfect mom."

If this is how you feel as you enter your third trimester, you're not alone. The third trimester is less "glowy goddess" and more "emotional mama bear with a to-do list."

This is the season when your body feels like it's preparing for both a miracle and a marathon. Your back aches, your sleep takes a nosedive, and you suddenly have a very strong opinion about stroller wheel alignment. One minute you're folding tiny onesies and weeping at a diaper commercial; the next, you're trying to Google "What does it mean if I just cried because I have to pee every five minutes?"

This chapter is here to catch you. No judgment. No pressure to "cherish every moment." Just real talk, helpful info, and a little humor to carry you through the swollen ankles, baby kicks to the bladder, checking the toilet paper after every wipe to make sure the mucus plug is still intact, and yes, whatever that mysterious craving you may have at 2 a.m.

## What's Actually Happening

Let's normalize the real ride from "Oh, wow, she's hiccuping!" to "Why does my pelvis feel like it's breaking in half?"

The third trimester is a wild mash-up of magic and mayhem. Sometimes, you're marveling at tiny kicks and hiccups; other times, you're googling "can your belly button pop off?" This stage is full of surprising milestones, some sweet, some weird, and some downright uncomfortable.

This isn't just about counting weeks and measuring belly growth. It's about everything your body, brain, and heart are doing behind the scenes as you edge closer to meeting your baby.

### Weeks 28–31: The Calm Before the Cramps

As you go through the third trimester, everything starts to feel a bit more crowded in your tummy. Your baby is now the size of an eggplant, and while they're busy working on brain folds and blinking, you're probably just trying to figure out how to sleep with six strategically placed pillows (Wahlberg, 2025).

Right now, your baby is fine-tuning important skills. Their brain is developing grooves and folds. It's almost like it's upgrading from a flip phone to a smartphone. They're also learning how to blink, their eyesight is sharpening (they still mostly see shadows), and their kicks are officially strong enough to make you gasp for air.

Hormones are once again doing the most. You might feel euphoric one moment and overwhelmed the next, especially as thoughts of labor start creeping in. You might also start to have some wild dreams, from giving birth to a cat to running a baby-themed obstacle course. Your brain is doing its best to work through the emotions you're not even consciously processing.

This is usually when your doctor will schedule your glucose screening test, the infamous sweet drink and blood draw to check for gestational diabetes (Boyd-Barrett, 2023). Is it fun? No. Is it important? Yes. If gestational diabetes goes unnoticed, it can lead to complications like a larger baby (hello, shoulder dystocia), early delivery, or even issues with your baby's blood sugar after birth. Catching it early means you and your doctor can make a plan to manage it safely.

You may also be checked for anemia, especially if you're feeling more drained than usual (Uscher, 2024). Anemia happens when your body doesn't have enough red blood cells to carry oxygen to your tissues, and growing a baby takes a lot of oxygen. If your iron levels are low, your doctor might suggest supplements or diet changes to keep your energy up and support healthy growth for the baby.

These are standard third-trimester checkpoints: nothing to fear, and everything to gain. They help your care team make sure both you and your baby are well-fueled, well-supported, and ready for the final stretch.

### You: Pillow Nests and Sleepless Nights

Sleep starts to feel like a vague concept you once believed in. Side-sleeping becomes the goal, but which side? For how long? And how does one keep a pillow between their knees, under their belly, and behind their back without becoming a human burrito?

- Invest in a C- or U-shaped pregnancy pillow. After the baby is born, you can use this as a feeding pillow as well (or continue to sleep with it, as it's just so comfortable).
- Pack different pillows around you to build a fortress. No joke, this helps.

- Magnesium lotion at night can help with leg cramps (and it feels fancy).
- Rotate sleeping spots if needed. This could be your couch, recliner, or wherever your hips don't scream.

Also, naps count. All naps. Especially the ones where you just "closed your eyes for a second" and woke up two hours later with one shoe on.

### Weeks 32–35: The Pressure Is Real

Okay, real talk: This is the part of pregnancy when things start to feel... hefty. Not just physically (though yes, your belly now has its own gravitational pull), but emotionally and mentally, too. There's a baby-sized weight sitting on your bladder and your to-do list, and somehow both are making you pee a little.

Ever feel a sudden, sharp zinger down there that stops you in your tracks? That's lightning crotch (De Pietro, 2023). Yes, it's a real thing, and yes, whoever named it deserves a medal. It's caused by the baby pressing on sensitive nerves as they settle lower in your pelvis.

You may also notice more frequent Braxton Hicks contractions, those tightening sensations across your belly that make you pause midsentence or midsnack (Donaldson-Evans, 2025a). These are your uterus doing practice drills. They're usually irregular, not too painful (just uncomfortable), and go away with rest, movement, or hydration.

Then there's round ligament pain, that stretchy, pulling feeling on the sides of your belly or groin (Miles, 2022). As annoying as they can be, they're normal. Think of it as your body making space, again, for the ever-growing little human who seems determined to rearrange your organs daily.

This is when the emotional weight can hit hard. Questions like *Will I be a good mom?*, *Do I have everything ready?* and *What if I forget how to swaddle?* swirl through your head. This is completely normal. The shift into "mom mode" often starts before birth. Let those thoughts come, and know that perfection isn't the goal. Love, presence, and showing up (even messy) are what matter.

If you haven't already, now's a good time to schedule your hospital or birth center tour. This gives you a chance to ask real questions (like, "Do you serve snacks?" and "What's your epidural policy?").

Start thinking about your pediatrician, too. Many offer short "meet and greets" so you can get a feel for their vibe. You're looking for someone who listens, communicates clearly, and makes you feel supported. (Bonus points if they don't bat an eye when you show up with mashed banana on your shirt.)

Birth classes can help ease some of the unknowns, whether you go for a classic in-person course, an online series you can watch in your pajamas, or a hypnobirthing podcast you fall asleep to nightly. There's no one right way to prepare, just what works for you.

Your body has changed a lot, and it's okay if that's affecting how you feel about sex, touch, or being seen naked. You might feel extra sensitive, disconnected, or the total opposite, randomly excited by even the slightest touch. Yes, my new mom friends, pregnancy is weird.

It can also be uncomfortable and downright difficult to find a sexual position that works while balancing your huge tummy. Open, gentle conversations with your partner can help you both stay emotionally connected, even if your sex life looks different for a while. This is a tender season. Be kind to yourself and each other.

By now, your doctor will likely start paying closer attention to your baby's position. Ideally, the baby is moving into the "head down" pose for birth, curled up with their head nestled in your pelvis like a little yogi. Don't panic if your baby is breech (butt or feet first). There's still time for them to flip, and your doctor may discuss options like exercises, chiropractic care, or even a gentle external version, if needed.

You can also start tuning in to how your baby moves. Kicks up high might mean a head-down baby, while kicks low could signal a different position. Either way, your care team will keep you informed and supported.

### Weeks 36–40: Welcome to the Waiting Game

You've made it to the final stretch. Your belly is stretched, your patience is stretched, and your underwear probably is, too. This is the home stretch, when time gets weird; somehow, the days drag and fly by all at once. One minute, you're folding baby socks and wondering whether you're actually nesting or just bored, and the next, you're crying because your partner forgot to buy the right kind of ice cream. This stage is full of excitement, nerves, mystery symptoms, and frequent bathroom trips.

As your body gears up for the big day, you might start wondering, *Is this it?* Or *am I just gassy?* (Real question. No shame.)

Here are a few common signs of early labor (Donaldson-Evans, 2025b):

- Mild cramping or period-like aches, especially in your lower back
- Increased pelvic pressure, like your baby's trying to elbow their way out
- Spotting or light bleeding, especially after a cervical check

- Loose stools and nausea (yep, it's a thing)
- More frequent and stronger Braxton Hicks that eventually form a pattern

But here's the kicker: Early labor can last hours... or days. And false alarms are common. You're not being dramatic if you call your doctor three times in one week. You're just in that beautifully frustrating place called "almost."

At some point, you might notice a globby, jelly-like discharge called the mucus plug. This is the seal that's been protecting your cervix, and when it comes out, it can be a sign that labor is near. But don't rush to the hospital just yet: Some moms-to-be lose their plugs a whole week before they go into labor.

If it's tinged with blood, that's called the bloody show (charming name, right?). That's usually a stronger hint that your cervix is changing and things could be picking up soon. Still, it's not a timer. It just means your body is doing something.

So, when do you call your doctor or midwife?

- If your water breaks (even if it's just a trickle)
- If contractions are strong, consistent, and getting closer together, apply the 5-1-1 rule: Your contractions should be 5 minutes apart, last 1 minute each, and continue for at least an hour
- If you experience heavy bleeding, decreased fetal movement, or just feel like something's not right

From Week 36 onward, you'll likely have weekly check-ins. These might include:

- Cervical checks to see whether you're dilated or effaced. (Spoiler: they don't always predict when labor will happen.)
- The Group B Strep (GBS) test, a quick swab to check for common bacteria (*Screening for Group B Strep Bacteria*, 2025). If you're positive, you'll get antibiotics during labor. It's nothing to stress about.
- Some providers may offer a membrane sweep (a gentle separation of the amniotic sac from your cervix) to try and nudge labor along once you're full term.

These appointments can feel like both a lifeline and a letdown. You're so close, but also... still pregnant.

It's okay if you're counting down the hours and clinging to the kicks. It's okay if you want your body back and feel overwhelmed by the thought of labor. This is a season of contradictions. You are allowed every feeling, even the messy ones.

I thought I was leaking jelly or something. Googled it at 2 a.m., and that's when I found out I had officially lost my mucus plug. Honestly, nothing could have prepared me for how gross and weirdly exciting that was!

**Decision Time: Where, How, and With Whom You'll Give Birth**

Birth is about the what (baby). It's also about the where, the how, and who will be by your side when it all goes down. Whether you dream of a hospital epidural ASAP, a cozy birth center vibe, or a water birth with fairy lights and calming playlists, your preferences matter.

This section is meant to help you feel safe, supported, and seen. You're allowed to ask questions, change your mind, and make choices that work for you. Let's explore your options and build a birth team that has your back, literally and emotionally.

*Choosing Where to Give Birth*

When it comes to birth, there's no one-size-fits-all answer. Some moms feel safest with monitors beeping and a full medical team nearby. Others want dim lights, essential oils, and someone rubbing their back while they labor in a birth tub. You get to choose what feels right to you, because this is your birth, your body, and your baby.

Let's explore the most common options.

**Hospital Birth**

**Pros:**

- Access to pain management (hello, epidural)
- Full medical team and emergency support on hand
- NICU access if needed
- Covered by most insurance plans

**Cons:**

- Less control over your environment and routines
- More interventions are possible (some necessary, some not)
- Staff can rotate, so there may be less continuity in care

Hospitals are a great choice for those who want medical reassurance, pain-relief options, or have higher-risk pregnancies. You can still bring comfort items, create a birth plan, and make the space your own.

.  .  .

BIRTH CENTER

**Pros:**

- Calmer, homier vibe than a hospital
- Focus on low-intervention, natural birth
- Supportive of movement, water birth, and birth preferences
- Midwife-led care with strong personal relationships

**Cons:**

- No epidural access (but there are tubs, massage, and snacks)
- Emergencies may require hospital transfer
- May or may not be covered by insurance

Birth centers are often a sweet spot: more comfort and freedom than a hospital, but still connected to medical backup if needed.

**Home Birth**

**Pros:**

- Maximum comfort, privacy, and control
- Familiar environment and uninterrupted bonding
- Personalized, continuous support from a midwife

**Cons:**

- Not ideal for high-risk pregnancies
- Pain relief is limited to natural methods
- Hospital transfer is required if complications arise
- Midwife services are often not covered by insurance

Home birth can be beautiful for those with uncomplicated pregnancies who feel safe and empowered in their own space. Midwives come equipped with skills and tools, but it's important to have a backup plan and a trusted care team.

**Money Talk: What's Covered?**

Before you fall in love with a dreamy birthing tub or high-tech hospital suite, double-check with your insurance provider:

- Ask which facilities and providers are in-network.
- Inquire about prenatal and postpartum coverage.
- Ask about coverage for midwives, doulas, and birth classes.

If you're paying out of pocket, birth centers and home births can be more affordable than a hospital delivery. It's worth comparing. Where you give birth is both a logistical and an emotional choice. What matters most to you?

- Do you feel safer with medical equipment nearby?
- Do you want more control over who's in the room and what your birth looks like?
- Do you thrive in calm, quiet environments?
- Do you want as few interventions as possible, or the full range of options?

There's no "right" answer. Just the one that makes you feel calm, confident, and cared for.

At first, I thought I had to pick whatever my doctor suggested. But once I toured the birth center and met the midwives, something clicked. I finally felt like I had a say in how my baby would be born, my husband didn't have too much of an opinion on it.

*Forming Your Dream Team*

Giving birth is powerful, beautiful, raw, intense, and slightly bananas. You deserve a crew that holds you up through every breath, push, and panic-snack in between.

It's your choice whom you want in the room with you, not just physically, but emotionally. Because labor is much more than contractions and cervix checks. You need to feel safe, seen, and supported as you bring a whole human into the world.

Some moms want a full squad: partner, doula, mom, sister, and maybe even their yoga teacher. Others want one calm person and as few voices as possible. Some give birth with a best friend on FaceTime, a playlist, or with their inner strength guiding the way.

There's no wrong way to build your dream team, just the way that's right for you.

## How to Build a Support Circle That Reflects *You*

You don't have to choose the "standard" lineup. There is no standard. Families come in all shapes, and so do birth teams. Here are a few real-mom dream-team combos:

- Sam, a single mom, chose her sister and a birth doula who specialized in trauma-informed care. "One expert to guide me and one snack carrier. That's all I needed."
- Jules and Dani, an LGBTQ+ couple, leaned on their midwife and a queer-friendly birth center to create a space where they felt affirmed and empowered.
- Anastacia, whose partner was deployed, set up a virtual support plan: FaceTime during early labor, voice memos from her patner, and her mom reading her affirmations out loud when things got intense.

Who's on your list?

- Someone to hold your hand (or remind you to unclench your jaw)
- Someone who knows when to speak and when to *shhh*
- Someone calm in chaos, and who doesn't take your yelling personally

Have a real conversation with your support people ahead of time. Say what you'll need emotionally, not just physically. How deeply your support shows up for you is what matters most.

**Partner Prep: From Awkward Silence to Emotional MVP**

Let's be honest: Some partners crush it in the delivery room. Others bring Uno cards "just in case."

If you've got a partner, it's never too early to help them step into their *Emotionally Available Partner Energy.*

What helps:

- **Practice comfort techniques together.** Try breathing, massage, or timing fake contractions on a lazy Sunday. It's weirdly bonding.
- **Talk through birth scenarios.** What do you hope they'll say or do if labor slows down? What if you want to change the plan?
- **Watch birth videos together.** Yep. Even the gross ones. It's real life, baby.
- **Direct them to bonus resources.** Perhaps *You Will Rock as a Dad!* (shameless plug, but hey, there's a checklist and everything).

Partners can be incredible sources of calm, courage, and connection during birth. They just need a little guidance, and sometimes permission, to show up emotionally, not just logistically.

Birth isn't a solo sport. But it is your game to lead. You get to choose your team, your tools, and your vibe. And when things get real, and they will, you'll know you've got the right people in your corner cheering you on. Holding space. Passing the water bottle. And reminding you that you were made for this.

**Hospital Bag and Final Essentials: What You'll Really Need**

Let's pack confidence and, of course, nipple balm.

As you approach the finish line, there's something deeply satisfying about packing that hospital bag. It's like prepping for a weird, life-altering sleepover with contractions. This section is here to help you separate the Pinterest-perfect packing lists from what you'll reach for at 3 a.m. with mesh undies halfway down your thighs.

Because when it comes to birth and baby prep, less is often more, except when it comes to snacks.

*The Real Hospital Bag Checklist*

This isn't just a checklist. It's a sanity-saver. Let's break it down into two piles: your stuff and your baby's stuff.

**For You**

- A long phone charger (those outlets are always five feet too far away)
- Flip-flops for the shower (trust us)
- Lip balm, hair ties, and face wipes. Labor is a sweaty business

- Comfy clothes for post-birth lounging (think: soft, loose, and dark-colored in case of leaks). Also, if you're planning on breastfeeding, look for button-up tops for easy access. You'll spend more time with your boobs hanging out than you've ever imagined
- Adult diapers or maternity pads (yes, really)
- Nipple balm (whether you're breastfeeding or not, just in case)
- Your pillow (with a nonwhite pillowcase so it doesn't get mixed up with hospital or clinic bedding)
- Snacks: protein bars, trail mix, hard candies, anything that says "I survived this day and earned sugar"
- Your normal toiletries
- A folder or envelope for paperwork
- Your birth plan (if you have one) and insurance info

## For Your Baby

- A going-home outfit (weather-appropriate and easy to get on)
- A swaddle or blanket for the ride home
- A pacifier, if you plan to use one (hospitals may not provide them)
- Optional: a special hat, bow, or keepsake for photos
- A car seat, installed and ready to go (more on that below!)

## What the Hospital Usually Provides

- Diapers and wipes
- Pads and mesh undies
- Baby blankets and a hat
- Formula, if needed
- Peri bottle, pain relievers, and other postpartum supplies

I packed four nursing bras, two robes, a portable fan, and a birthing playlist. What did I use? A phone charger, lip balm, and the extra underwear I almost left out. Pack light, you will want to bring a million things but you won't need it.

### Must-Have Gear Before Baby Arrives

You've probably been bombarded with product ads and nursery tours worthy of *Architectural Digest*. Breathe. You don't need to own a baby wipe warmer or a diaper pail that syncs with Bluetooth.

Let's talk real-deal essentials, the things that matter when baby comes home:

- **Car seat:** You can't leave the hospital without it. Practice installing it early. Many local fire stations or hospitals offer car seat checks. Rear-facing, in the back seat, and tightly secured is the best way to keep your precious little bundle safe and sound.
- **Safe sleep setup:** A bassinet or crib with a firm mattress and no extras (no pillows, bumpers, or stuffed animals). Keeping it boring means keeping it safe.
- **Changing area:** Whether it's a full table or just a basket with diapers and wipes next to your bed, make it work for you. Bonus points for having a second setup in another room, for example, the family room, where you'll spend a lot of time with your baby.
- **Laundry prep:** Wash baby's clothes, blankets, and swaddles in baby-safe detergent. Spoiler alert: Baby laundry is constant.
- **Swaddles and sleepers:** A few soft, easy-to-zip sleepers and some swaddles (Velcro ones are lifesavers at 2 a.m.). You don't need 27, unless you don't plan on doing any laundry over the first month.

- **Feeding support:** Whether you're nursing, pumping, or bottle-feeding, get the basics ready: a nursing pillow, bottles, nipple cream, or formula you've researched and feel good about.
- **Monitor (optional):** Some parents swear by them. Others keep the baby nearby and wing it. Choose based on your comfort, not pressure.

You're about to do something amazing. Whether your bag is color-coded or half-zipped with a pack of granola bars and hope, it's enough. You're enough. And hey, if you forget something, you can always rely on your partner, the hospital, or your favorite humans (make sure someone has a key to your home to fetch anything you might need). You've got this.

You've sorted through your fears, picked your team, and packed your bag, but now comes the part no one can truly prepare you for: the moment your body says, "It's time."

Labor doesn't follow a script. It might be loud or silent, fast or slow, calm or chaotic. But you deserve to enter it feeling informed and supported, not scrambling for Google at 3 a.m. In the next chapter, we'll break down the signs, stages, and surprises of labor, not with medical jargon, but with the kind of real-talk wisdom you'd get from a best friend who's been there. Because this isn't just the end of pregnancy.

It's the beginning of everything.

# 5

## BIRTH DAY IS NOT JUST ONE DAY

They say giving birth is like running a marathon. But here's the catch: You don't know the route, there's no set start time, and your training plan keeps changing. Oh, and the finish line might move by a week or two (or more). More than 50% of first-time moms go past their due date, and yet somehow, the pressure to be "ready" by week 36 feels like a ticking clock (Dekker, 2017).

Labor is a physical event and a mindset shift. It's standing on the edge of something powerful, mysterious, and completely life-changing. No one else can walk this path for you, but you're not leaping into the unknown alone.

This chapter is here to help you make sense of the chaos: what's normal (spoiler: a lot), what might surprise you, and how to ride the waves with more confidence, no matter when or how labor begins.

You've made it to the threshold. Let's take the next step together.

COUNTDOWN MODE (WEEKS 36–42)

Welcome to the waiting game, also known as the final boss level of pregnancy. You're officially in the window in which your baby could arrive any day... or not for several more weeks. It's the ultimate lesson in surrender: Your to-do list is screaming, your body is groaning, and your brain is ping-ponging between "I'm so ready" and "Wait, am I ready?!"

These final weeks are full of subtle shifts, some physical, some emotional, but all very real. We'll walk you through what to expect, feel, track, and prep as your due date approaches (and possibly passes). Whether you're riding steady or counting every Braxton Hicks like a stopwatch, we've got tools, tips, and encouragement to help you navigate this stretch with more calm and confidence.

### Baby's Almost Here: What's Happening Inside

While you're pacing, prepping, and possibly Googling "how to induce labor naturally," your baby is still hard at work finishing their final touches. Just because you're full term doesn't mean the baby's ready yet. These last few weeks are like backstage prep before opening night. A lot is happening behind the scenes.

Inside the womb, your baby is fine-tuning systems that will help them thrive in the outside world. Their brain is developing at lightning speed. Lungs are maturing so they can take that first breath. Fat stores are building to regulate body temperature. And reflexes like sucking, swallowing, and gripping are getting stronger every day.

Even if you feel ready to meet your little one (or just to see your feet again), every extra day inside gives them more strength, coordination, and grit. Here's what your baby's working on, week by week:

### Week 36: Almost There

Your baby is about the size of a papaya and weighs around 6.2 pounds (Blanding, 2024). Lungs are still maturing, but getting close to full function. The digestive system is nearly ready, although it won't kick into full gear until after birth. Your baby is shedding the last of the fine hair (lanugo) and protective wax (vernix) that's coated their skin. They're also practicing sucking, blinking, and breathing.

### Week 37: Full Term (Sort of)

As of this week, your baby is considered early term. They're still working on fat stores (chubby cheeks incoming). The lungs and brain are continuing to mature, and their grip is strong enough to hold your finger. Baby may also start moving down into your pelvis, which can make breathing easier for you, but also add new pressure down below and on your bladder. Fun times.

### Week 38: Practicing for Showtime

Baby's organs are fully formed, and they're now just refining and practicing all the things they'll need on the outside: breathing rhythmically, sucking, swallowing, and stretching. The brain and nervous system development are still ongoing (and will be for years!), but the basics are in place. Your baby might be less squirmy and more curled up due to the tight space.

### Week 39: Full Term, For Real

Welcome to the official full term! Your baby now weighs 7–8 pounds on average and is about the size of a mini-watermelon (Burch, 2024). Their lungs are ready to breathe air, and their brain is still growing fast. Fat continues to build, which will help with temperature regulation after birth. They're also building immunity, borrowing antibodies from you as a starter immune system.

**Week 40: Due Date! (But Baby's Calendar Might Differ)**

Most babies don't actually arrive on their due date, but that doesn't mean this week isn't important. Your baby is still soaking in the benefits of your womb: warmth, antibodies, and a gentle transition to the noisy, bright world waiting outside.

**Weeks 41–42: Bonus Round**

If your baby is fashionably late, try not to panic. Many first-time moms go beyond 40 weeks. As long as the baby is being monitored and everything looks healthy, it's perfectly okay to wait it out. In these extra days, your baby continues to build fat and develop brain connections. You'll likely have more check-ins with your doctor to track fluid levels, placenta function, and baby's movements, but chances are, your little one is just taking their sweet time.

*Your Body's Subtle Countdown Signals*

By this point, you might feel like a detective trying to read your own body's clues. Every twinge, cramp, and bathroom trip sparks the question: Is this it? And the answer, infuriatingly, is mostly either a hopeful maybe or a clear no.

The truth is, your body doesn't flip a switch into labor. It warms up gradually, sending little signals that change day by day. Some are physical. Some are emotional. Some are so subtle you might miss them entirely unless you're paying close attention (and, let's be real, you probably are).

One of the more noticeable signs is when your baby "drops," or settles lower into your pelvis. This shift, often called lightning, can happen a few weeks before labor starts, especially if it's your first baby. You might suddenly be able to breathe easier, but also feel like you're waddling through molasses. Increased pressure on your bladder, hips, and lower back is totally normal and a sign that things are shifting in the right direction.

You might also notice an uptick in energy or, conversely, feel completely wiped out. Some moms get a strong urge to clean, organize, or prep everything in sight (I'm sure you know all about the nesting instinct by now). Others can barely make it through the day without a nap and a snack every 10 minutes. Both ends of the spectrum are completely normal. It's just your body responding to major hormonal changes as it gets ready for the main event.

Then there are the emotional signals: mood swings, sudden tears, strange dreams, or just an overwhelming sense that something is coming. These waves might catch you off guard, but try not to brush them off. They're part of your internal shift from pregnancy to parenthood. Your body isn't the only thing preparing. Your whole being is.

Internally, your cervix may also be making slow, quiet progress. You might be effacing (thinning out) or dilating (opening) without even feeling it. Some people walk around partially dilated for weeks, while others show zero progress until labor kicks in full force. It's not a performance metric. It's just your body doing its own thing, in its own time.

You'll remember the mucus plug we mentioned in the previous chapter. If you haven't already seen it yet, losing it (or noticing a "bloody show") can be another hint that your cervix is softening and opening. It's not a green light for labor, but it means things are starting to happen behind the scenes.

Meanwhile, your uterus might be throwing in some practice rounds. Braxton Hicks contractions are common in the final weeks. They're usually irregular, don't increase in intensity, and tend to fade with rest or hydration. Think of them as warm-up stretches. They're different from true labor contractions, which grow stronger, longer, and closer together over time. An easy test to determine whether you're experiencing Braxton Hicks or the real deal is to move around. Braxton Hicks will disappear while you're moving, while active labor will just continue to get stronger.

If your water breaks, whether it's a big gush or a slow trickle, or if you notice a sudden decrease in your baby's movements, don't wait to call your doctor. Also, reach out if you have bright-red bleeding, intense pain that doesn't come and go, or just a gut feeling that something's not right. You don't need to talk yourself out of concern or wait until it feels "urgent enough." You're allowed to ask questions and get reassurance.

Finally, a note on your water breaking: It doesn't usually happen like it does in the movies. Sometimes it's a dramatic gush, but often it's more of a confusing trickle. It may be hard to tell whether it's amniotic fluid or something else. Don't worry: You won't be the first to call your doctor and ask, "Did I just pee myself, or...?" They've heard it all.

So, yes, your body is talking to you. Some days, it'll be a whisper; other days, it'll feel like a shout. You don't have to interpret every signal perfectly. You just have to trust that something beautiful is beginning. One way or another, baby is on their way, and you'll know when it's time.

### Checklist: How to Mentally Prepare When Nothing Feels Predictable

- **Remind yourself: Birth isn't a test you have to pass.**
  There's no "right" way to do this, only *your* way.
- **Make a plan, and be ready to toss it.** Having preferences

is great. Just hold them loosely. Your baby might have their own ideas.

- **Practice surrendering control in small ways.** Let someone else pack the diaper bag. Skip the perfect freezer meals. Flexing this muscle now helps later.

- **Learn the stages of labor so you feel less surprised.** Understanding what might happen helps you feel more grounded, even if your path winds differently.

- **Choose a mantra you can come back to.** "I am safe." "One wave at a time." "My body knows what to do." Keep it short and calming.

- **Line up your support team, and let them know what helps.** Whether it's a partner, doula, or BFF, let them know how to be your anchor.

- **Get curious instead of scared.** When things shift, try asking, "What's my body doing now?" instead of "Is this bad?"

- **Accept that fear might show up, and that's okay.** You can be scared and strong. The two can exist side by side.

- **Trust that you'll figure it out moment by moment.** You don't need to know everything now. You'll meet each stage when it arrives.

**What Labor Really Looks Like**

Forget the dramatic movie scenes where someone's water breaks and ten minutes later there's a baby. Real labor is usually slower, messier, and a lot more ordinary, and that's a good thing. It gives you time to settle in, breathe, and let your body lead.

Labor doesn't follow a script, but it does tend to unfold in stages, each with its own rhythm and purpose. Let's go through what those phases might feel like, physically, emotionally, and mentally, so you're not caught off guard when things shift. Spoiler: You're stronger than you think, and yes, you really can do this.

*The Phases of Labor (What to Expect in Each Stage)*

Labor is not one long scream followed by a baby and a lullaby. It's more like a series of strange, sacred, sweaty moments during which your body slowly opens up and your mind wonders how the heck you're supposed to be chill about it.

But there's a rhythm to the chaos. Labor typically unfolds in three main phases: early labor, active labor, and transition. Here's what each one might feel like. Just remember: No two births are exactly alike, and that's okay.

### Early Labor: "Is This... Something?"

This is the beginning, but it often doesn't feel like it. Contractions might be mild and irregular, like period cramps or a tight squeeze that comes and goes. It often starts with back pain rather than those typical abdominal contractions you expect to feel. You'll likely be able to eat, shower, walk around, and even nap (please nap if you can). It can last hours, or sometimes even days, especially if it's your first baby.

You might feel excited, impatient, or unsure if this is it. That's normal. This is a great time to hydrate, rest, and try to go about your day. Yes, it's happening, but no, you don't need to rush to the hospital just yet.

I texted my family group chat that I was in labor. Twenty-six hours later, I was still in early labor. One of them just replied, "LOL, rookie move."

Active Labor: "Oh, Okay, This Is Definitely Something"

Contractions become more regular, longer, and stronger. You're working now on getting closer to that magical (and frightening) push. You may need to breathe through them. It might feel like intense cramps that build to a peak, then ease off, like waves coming in faster and harder. You might not feel chatty anymore, and that's a sign things are progressing.

Your doctor might recommend heading in around this stage, depending on the timing of your contractions (remember the 5-1-1 rule?). Things are intensifying, but you're not alone. You've got a team, tools, and breath.

**Transition: "Everyone Leave Me Alone. But Also Stay."**

This is the most intense, shortest phase, also known as the final push (literally) of your pregnancy. Your cervix dilates from around 7 to 10 cm, and things can feel wild. You might shake, cry, vomit, swear, or say things you'll later blame on the hormones (and rightly so). It's common to say, "I can't do this anymore." But you can. And you are doing it.

This is the deep end of labor, but it's also the doorway. Once you're through it, you'll start pushing, and then, finally, meet your baby.

**Normal Labor Side Effects**

No one talks about these enough:

- Shaking like you're freezing (your body's response to hormones)
- Feeling nauseous or vomiting (yes, you might not be able to waddle to the bathroom in time, so best to keep a bucket close by)

- Crying for no reason, sometimes from fear, sometimes from relief
- The sudden urge to poop (because baby's head is right there pressing on your rectum!)

All of it? Completely normal. Welcome to labor.

**To Epidural or Not to Epidural?**

You're not less brave if you get one, or more magical if you don't. Here's the breakdown:

**Pros:**

- Pain relief (like, real, genuine, amazing relief)
- It can help you rest if labor is long
- It can make you feel more in control

**Cons:**

- You'll experience numbness or reduced mobility
- It might slow labor in some cases
- It might reduce your ability to push your baby out
- Rare but possible side effects (like low blood pressure or headaches)

**Common epidural myths:**

- **You can't feel anything.** Not true at all! You'll probably still feel pressure and the urge to push. Your doctor might also turn the epidural off when it's crunch time so that you can feel those final contractions to know when to push without tearing.

- **It always leads to a C-section.** Not at all. Many women have successful vaginal deliveries after an epidural.
- **You can't move at all.** There are low-dose options (sometimes called "walking epidurals") that allow some mobility. Otherwise, just enjoy the rest. You'll need it for the final push.

**Other pain-management options:**

- **Birthing ball:** Sit, sway, and bounce helps the baby move down and opens the pelvis.
- **Water birth or tub labor:** Warm water can ease tension and pain.
- **Hypnobirthing:** Breathing and visualization can help you focus.
- **Movement:** Walking, squatting, and rocking can all help to rope in your new best friend: gravity.
- **Counter-pressure or massage:** Especially if you're having back labor. This is when you feel most of the contraction pain in your lower back instead of (or in addition to) your belly. It can feel like intense, constant pressure or like your spine is staging a protest. This often happens when the baby is facing up (sunny-side up), with the back of their head pressing against your spine.

Bottom line: There is no gold medal for suffering. Do what feels right for you in the moment.

I had a very clear plan of being a tough cookie during labor. I wanted no pain meds whatsoever. I figured my body was made for labor. But, after hours in labor and still only being 6 cm dilated, I couldn't anymore. And, within 30 minutes of getting an epidural, I was at 9 cm and almost ready to push. It was magical.

**What About C-Sections?**

Sometimes babies take the scenic route or need a new exit plan. A C-section might be planned (medical reasons or for a breech baby) or unplanned (when labor stalls or the baby goes into distress). Unless you planned to have a C-section, always remember this:

- C-sections are a form of childbirth. You're still becoming a mom.
- They are not a failure.
- Recovery is different, but you still grew and birthed a human. That's huge.

**Labor Fears No One Warned Me About**

Even the most prepared moms have that one thing they secretly dread. And guess what? You're not alone.

**Common quiet fears:**

- "What if I tear?"
- "What if I poop?"
- "What if I panic?"
- "What if it ends in an emergency C-section?"

Let's break those down.

- **Tearing happens:** Most of the time, it's minor. Your doctor can use warm compresses or hands-on techniques to minimize it. If the tear is major, you will need stitches, but these are inserted so quickly, you'll barely notice them. You'll likely be distracted by your adorable newborn, anyway.

- **Pooping during birth is very common:** No one will flinch. Truly. Your birth team handles it like brushing lint off your shirt. It means you're pushing effectively! So, you actually deserve a badge of honor for pooping on the delivery table. It's effectively a rite of passage to motherhood.
- **Fear of losing control:** Labor can feel raw and primal, but that doesn't mean you're not doing it right. If you feel overwhelmed, that doesn't mean you're failing. It means you're human.
- **Emergency birth scenarios:** It's scary when plans have to change suddenly, especially when you hear the word "emergency" used. But remember that birth teams are trained for this. You won't be alone. Ask questions and voice your fears. Your doctor wants you to feel safe and heard.

Your experience doesn't have to look like anyone else's. You don't have to float in a candlelit tub or deliver in 12 minutes to have a beautiful story. Your labor will be powerful because you lived it. That's enough.

I watched 17 birth vlogs and was convinced I'd scream the whole time. Instead, I quietly whispered "ow" for like five hours, but believe me it was still not pretty.

*What You Might Not Expect*

So the baby's out, right? Champagne and snuggles? Not quite yet.

After the delivery, your body still has one more job: the placenta. Yes, you'll need to push one more time, though this part is usually quick and less intense.

You might still shake or feel a wave of emotions. Some moms need stitches. Some feel overwhelmed by joy, or nothing at all, right away. It's all normal.

Then comes skin-to-skin, if all is well. These are those magical first minutes when your baby is placed on your chest, learning your smell, your heartbeat, and your voice. You might even be encouraged to try breastfeeding your baby. This is often called the golden hour, when time blurs and bonding begins.

Meanwhile, your baby will get a quick check (Apgar scores, vitals, and first cry), and you might notice your doctor pressing on your belly to help your uterus contract (often in a circular motion). Again: weird, but normal. Apart from helping your uterus contract, this gentle pressure also helps to get a lot of blood out, so the more they get out, the fewer maternity pads (or surfboards, as I used to call them) you'll have to wear afterward. Bonus!

If things get unexpected, maybe baby needs some breathing support, or your bleeding is heavier than expected, remember: Emergency doesn't always mean danger. It means attention, action, and care.

If you have a birth partner with you, this is their moment to shine, holding your hand, asking questions, and being your voice if you need one. Their job isn't to fix or direct. It's to be your anchor.

### Postpartum Starts During Labor

Most people think postpartum begins the moment the baby is born, but in reality, it starts the moment you begin to stretch beyond who you were. The hours after birth are not just about the baby; they're the beginning of your recovery, your rebirth, and your fourth trimester.

The emotional shifts, the physical aftermath, and the raw tenderness of those first days all begin while you're still in that delivery room. Yes, my new mom friends, postpartum is real, it matters, and you deserve care, too. Let's talk about what to expect when the world thinks your part is done, but you're just getting started.

### Welcome to the Fourth Trimester

No one really warns you that the moment the baby's born, you don't get magically "unpregnant." You're still swollen, leaking, sore, and running on love and adrenaline (with maybe a little fear).

The fourth trimester, those first 12 weeks after birth, isn't about "bouncing back." It's about healing, adjusting, and becoming. It's a time of hormonal shifts, identity shifts, and more bodily fluids than you thought possible. And yes, you deserve all the snacks, support, and slow mornings you can get.

### What to Expect (Besides a Baby)

- **Mesh underwear:** No, they aren't glamorous, but they can be surprisingly comfortable. Most hospitals will give you a few to use.
- **Padsicles:** These are frozen witch hazel pads or premade "cooling" pads. They feel like heaven after vaginal birth. DIY tip: Freeze maxi pads with aloe and witch hazel in zip lock bags before you go into labor.
- **Stool softeners:** No one wants to talk about this, but you'll thank yourself later. Your first postpartum poop can be a spiritual journey. Don't skip the softeners.
- **Leaking everything:** Milk, sweat, and tears are all leaking out of you. You're a waterfall of life right now.

Nothing humbles you like waddling to the bathroom in mesh

undies and spritzing your lady parts with a peri bottle. I was like, "So this is motherhood, huh?"

**Prepare Mentally (Not Just With Stuff)**

Labor prep is great, but postpartum prep is next-level wisdom. While it's difficult to know how to prepare until your baby is there, here are three things to consider:

- **Slow down.** You don't have to host visitors, respond to texts, or be "on." Your job is healing and bonding.
- **Say no.** This can be to surprise guests, questions like "When are you going to start sleep training?" or anything that makes you clench your jaw.
- **Build a support team.** Think doulas, lactation consultants, meal trains, or friends who bring food without expecting small talk. Ask for help before you need it.

**Couples: Talk Now, Love Later (Just Kidding... Talk *and* Love Now)**

You're both about to be cracked open by this experience in different ways. Talk now about what might come after:

- Who's doing nighttime diaper changes?
- How will you check in with each other emotionally?
- What's one small thing that helps you feel seen when you're overwhelmed, tired, or teary?

Hint: It's okay if neither of you has all the answers. It's the talking that builds the bridge.

. . .

THE FIRST 24–48 HOURS: **The Truth**

- You might shake, cry, feel euphoric, or weirdly detached.
- You might stare at your baby like, "Who are you?"
- Your body might feel hollow, raw, powerful, and alien all at once.

All of it is normal. Birth may be over, but your transformation has only just begun.

### *Congratulations! This Is Your Next Chapter*

Giving birth is not the final scene. It's the first page of a brand-new story. Your body did something monumental, but now your mind and heart are catching up. You are not expected to instantly know how to be a mom. You're expected to show up, love fiercely, and figure it out one weird, beautiful day at a time.

When you have a free minute, write about what you'd most want to remember about your baby's birth. Write it on a napkin, in your phone notes, or in a notebook. You'll want to come back to this moment someday.

There might be moments of fear, doubt, or fog. You might feel overwhelmed. That doesn't mean you're doing it wrong. It means you care. It means you're in it. You'll learn more in Chapter 6 about postpartum mental health, but here's your gentle preview: If things feel off, you are not alone. If you need help, it doesn't mean you're weak. And if all you can do is hold your baby and breathe through the unknown, that's enough.

### *The Emotional Aftershock*

Childbirth is a full-body, full-heart earthquake. After the intensity, the quiet can feel oddly strange. Some moms feel a birth high or an oxytocin-fueled euphoria. Others crash into exhaustion, confusion, or flat-out weepiness. Most feel a little bit of everything.

**What's Totally Normal:**

- Crying even when you're happy
- Feeling anxious or protective
- Missing your pregnant belly (yes, really)
- Feeling disconnected from your baby, or overly attached and scared to let them out of your sight
- Thinking, *What have I done?* and *I love this tiny human so much it hurts* in the same hour

**Don't Go Through It Alone**

Love often grows slowly, like a candle instead of a firework. Some moms fall instantly, others take days or weeks. What matters is showing up. The bond will come. And, always remember that you don't have to do it alone:

- Text another mom friend who gets it.
- Join a local or online support group.
- Just hearing "same here" can be life-giving.

Even when it feels like everything is shifting, trust this: You've never done this before, but your love is not new. It's been waiting for this moment. And now, it gets to grow with your baby.

I kept waiting for the movie moment when I'd burst into tears and whisper, "I love you." Instead, I looked at my baby and said, "Okay, so you're mine now?" Love came later. It was still real.

❧

YOU DID IT. Whether birth went according to plan or flipped upside down, you crossed the biggest threshold of your life. Now what? In the next chapter, we walk through the beautiful mess that is the fourth trimester: healing, bonding, feeding, and redefining yourself one raw, sacred day at a time.

# 6

# YOU'RE A MAMA NOW, GENTLE HEALING, FIERCE LOVE

They hand you a baby, but no one hands you a guide for putting yourself back together. Not emotionally, physically, or even logistically (seriously, where's the instruction manual for breastfeeding while crying and holding a peri bottle?).

The postpartum phase involves more than recovery. It's a reckoning. With your body. With your identity. With the breathtaking, bone-deep love that now takes up residence in your chest.

This chapter is your reminder: Healing is not the opposite of strength. Slowing down is not weakness. Asking for help is not failure.

You just brought life into the world. Now, let's talk about how you begin caring for the one who made that possible: you.

### From Hospital Bed to Home Base

You might leave the hospital (or birth center) with a tiny, hat-wearing human, a vague reminder to follow up in six weeks, and a plastic bag filled with mesh underwear. What you don't leave with is a detailed guide for managing the tidal wave of emotions, hormones, healing, and logistics that hits the moment you step out those sliding doors.

Coming home with a baby is breathtaking and also disorienting. You're not just leaving a medical facility. You're leaving behind a team that was monitoring you around the clock. Now, suddenly, you're the one in charge of this tiny person as well as your own healing. It's a shift so big, it deserves more than just a "congrats" and a car seat.

This next stretch is tender and real. It's where everything starts to unfold.

### What No One Tells You About Discharge Day

Discharge day is often a strange blur of forms, diapers, and fragile feelings. You're given paperwork about newborn care while sitting on an ice pack, and somehow expected to absorb it all with a brain that's still swimming in adrenaline and oxytocin.

You might cry on the way home. Or laugh. Or sit in stunned silence, wondering how the heck they're letting you leave with a whole human. And then you walk into your home. The same home you left, but everything has changed. You are no longer just you. You are now a parent.

That invisible transition hits hard. The walls look familiar, but you feel brand new and slightly inside-out. For your partner or support person, this is the time to:

- Handle as much of the logistics as possible (think car seat wrangling, discharge paperwork, and snack-fetching).
- Watch your face for signs of "I'm okay" masking "I'm overwhelmed."

- Offer calm reassurance without pressure: "Take your time, we've got this."

**What's normal in those first 24 hours?**

- Crying for no reason
- Laughing at weird things
- Feeling like you're floating through someone else's life
- Wondering when it'll "feel real"

Whatever you feel, it's valid.

**Gentle mantra for the ride home:** This is big, but you're doing it and you'll be just fine.

### *The First 72 Hours of Postpartum Reality*

Okay, deep breath. We're going to get real here, because those first few days are a wild, sacred mess. Your body is in recovery mode: You're bleeding, leaking, sweating, possibly stitched up, and trying to figure out how to feed a baby while remembering how to sit without wincing.

That first bathroom trip might even feel Oscar-worthy. You deserve applause. Maybe even a cookie. You'll pee sideways, spray warm water with a peri bottle, dab instead of wipe, and possibly feel like your organs are free-floating. It's all okay. It's all part of it.

The biggest tip I can give you here is to set boundaries early. Your front door will likely be busier than the airport's arrival gate. Visitors will mean well. They might even bring muffins. But unless they're also bringing gentle energy, a casserole, or a willingness to do laundry, you get to say no. Your healing and bonding time comes first. Another thing: You can also absolutely insist that everyone washes their hands and turn away anyone who just looks like they might be sniffing. You're in mom-mode now, whether you actually feel like a mom or not. And it's your job to look out for your little one's health and safety.

### Your Partner's Role in This Chapter

Partners, listen up! This isn't just her recovery. It's your chapter, too. Here's how to show up in all the right ways:

- **Advocate for her rest.** If she's trying to "be a good host" or insists on doing laundry, remind her that she just gave birth. Her only job is to heal and bond.
- **Offer emotional support without fixing.** It's okay if you don't have answers. "That sounds hard. I'm here with you" is often enough.
- **Share the load.** That means diapers, dishes, middle of the night burping, and noticing when she hasn't had a warm meal.
- **Say the little things.** "You're doing so well." "I'm proud of you." "Want me to hold the baby while you shower?"

### Scripts That Help

Some partners quickly catch on to the enormity of the whole experience. Others may need a gentle nudge (or a giant push, if you're not carrying stitches, of course). Here are a few lines that can help:

- "Can you take the baby while I cry, eat, or nap?"
- "I need help with $X$, even if I don't know exactly how to ask."
- "Please check in on me, even when I say I'm fine."

Because here's the truth: Healing happens more gently when the person doing the healing feels seen.

**Your Body, Rewritten**

No one warns you that your body might feel like it's been hit by a bus, and yet, you also just ran the marathon of your life. Welcome to the paradox of postpartum.

This part of motherhood is often skipped over in baby books, blurred out in the highlight reels, and whispered about instead of said out loud. But you deserve the truth, not to scare you, but to prepare you.

Your body has done something extraordinary. And now, it's doing something just as powerful: healing. Let's walk through it, one honest, unfiltered moment at a time.

*Physical Recovery: Vaginal and Cesarean*

Whether you delivered vaginally, had a planned C-section, or ended up with an unplanned one after hours of labor, your recovery matters. None of it is "easy," and all of it is worthy of care, rest, and support.

Here's what you might encounter in the first few weeks:

- **Stitches or tearing:** You might feel sore, raw, or tender. Spray bottles (peri bottles) become your new BFF: aim, spray, dab (don't wipe), and repeat.
- **Incision care for C-sections:** Keep it clean, dry, and protected. It might feel numb or tingly. You might walk like a crab. That's okay. You might also struggle to pick your baby up. Ask your partner, BFF, or willing family member for help.

- **Belly binders:** Some moms swear by them for core support. Others toss them after Day 2. Listen to your body.
- **Medications:** If you're in pain, ask for help. This isn't the time to be a hero. Pain relief is a form of self-respect. You've been through enough already.

Oh, and let's say this again, clearly and loudly so that those stubborn people at the back can also hear it: C-sections aren't cheating or taking the easy way out. It's major abdominal surgery and postpartum recovery rolled into one. That is not for the faint of heart.

*What's Normal... and What's Not*

Your body may surprise you with its strange little rebellions. Some are normal, while others need attention. Let's break it down:

**Totally normal:**

- Night sweats so intense you think your water broke again
- Afterbirth cramps (especially during breastfeeding)
- Body odor that smells like a sweaty sports team slept on you
- Hair loss (It grows back, I promise.)

**When to check in with your doctor:**

- Bleeding that soaks through a pad in under an hour
- Foul-smelling discharge or fever
- Signs of prolapse: pressure, bulging, or heaviness "down there"
- Severe pain, swelling, or a bad feeling you just can't shake

Healing isn't linear. Some days you'll feel like you're flying. Others, like you're falling. Both are part of the process.

### Mental Health Checkpoint

This part is so important, yet it's often the quietest. Baby blues are common in the first two weeks. You may cry easily, feel weepy or overwhelmed, or swing between joy and sorrow like it's an Olympic event.

But if it lasts longer, gets worse, or you just don't feel like yourself, you could be facing postpartum depression or anxiety. And that's not your fault.

Let's talk about something even fewer people name: intrusive thoughts. Sudden, scary, uninvited ideas like, *What if I drop the baby?* or *What if something bad happens?* These are surprisingly common and not a sign you're unsafe or unfit. What matters is how you respond, and asking for support if they won't go away.

**Call your doctor or reach out if you:**

- Feel persistently sad, numb, or angry
- Feel disconnected from your baby
- Can't sleep even when the baby is sleeping
- Have thoughts of harming yourself or others

Always remember that you're not broken. You're brave. You're becoming.

### Reclaiming Your Self

There's a moment, maybe it's 3 a.m. during a feeding, when you wonder, *Where did I go?* Spoiler alert: You're still in there.

Motherhood expands you, but it doesn't erase you. It's not about "getting back to normal." It's about gently reclaiming who you are, one breath, one sip of water, or one sacred shower at a time.

### What Self-Care Looks Like Now

Forget the spa days and bubble baths from the Instagram version of "self-care." Right now, self-care is survival-care. It's small acts that remind your body, "I matter too."

Five-minute wins that actually help:

- Using the peri bottle like a pro
- Changing into fresh underwear
- Drinking a full glass of water
- Sitting down and putting your feet up
- Asking someone else to hold the baby while you stare at a wall for four minutes (you earned it)

### What Is a Sitz Bath?

A sitz bath is a warm, shallow bath that gently soaks your perineal area (yep, the space between your vagina and anus). It's magic for:

- Reducing swelling
- Soothing stitches or tears
- Hemorrhoid relief (I know, I know)
- Promoting healing after vaginal birth

You can sit in a clean bathtub with a few inches of warm (not hot!) water, or use a small plastic basin that fits over your toilet. Add Epsom salt, witch hazel, or just keep it simple. Then breathe, relax, and heal.

## THE SACRED SHOWER

Let's not underestimate what a few minutes under warm water can do for your soul. It's not just about getting clean. It's about remembering you're human. That you exist outside of feedings and diapers.

You might cry in there. You might mentally rehearse clap backs to someone who said, "Sleep when the baby sleeps." Either way, you're processing, and that counts.

### Body Image and That Stranger in the Mirror

"I don't recognize myself." If you've whispered this while staring at your belly, your breasts, and your tired eyes, you're not alone. Your body grew and birthed a human. You're allowed to grieve, adjust, and feel a little lost as you learn to love this new version of yourself.

Try this: Instead of asking, "How do I look?" Ask, "What did I just survive?" Then say thank you to your body.

### Reframing Rest

Lying down is not laziness. It's resistance against a world that tries to rush you through recovery. Every time you choose rest, you're choosing healing over hustle. And that's powerful.

### Nutrition Basics That Don't Involve Cooking

- **Hydration:** Keep a water bottle within arm's reach at all times; bonus points if it has a straw
- **Iron-rich foods:** Think lentils, spinach, fortified cereals, or a spoonful of peanut butter
- **Easy protein:** Hard-boiled eggs, yogurt, trail mix, a slice of cheese—no judgment if it's in your robe pocket
- **Mood support:** Oats, bananas, and yes, dark chocolate

Eat what you can, when you can. Some days, a handful of crackers *is* the victory.

### Moving Again, Gently

Forget the pressure to "bounce back." You're not a beach ball. You are a woman who just moved mountains with her body.

Most doctors say light walking is fine once you're home and comfortable. But "movement" can also mean breathing deeply while lying down, or stretching your arms while holding your baby. Here are a few things to consider:

- **Pelvic floor care:** Whether you had a vaginal or cesarean birth, your pelvic floor worked overtime. Ask your doctor about pelvic floor therapy or gentle Kegels. Peeing when you laugh is a sign that your body needs care.
- **Diastasis recti:** That's the fancy term for ab separation. Some moms notice a soft gap or bulge in the middle of their belly. Recovery takes time, and sometimes you may need a little extra help. Avoid crunches and consult a pro if you're unsure.
- **Red flags vs. green lights:**
- **Green light:** You feel energized after short walks with no pain or bleeding.
- **Red flag:** Heavy bleeding, dizziness, sharp pain, or pressure "down there." That's your sign to rest or call your doctor.

Let's look at a few gentle physical reminders:

- Sit tall when you feed the baby and add back support to make you comfortable.
- Roll out of bed sideways, not like a zombie rising.

- Breathe deeply into your belly at least once a day. It's grounding and healing.

### Menstruation, Hormones, and What's Happening Down There

Postpartum hormones are a carnival ride you didn't ask for. But let's demystify what's going on:

Your period might return:

- As soon as five weeks after giving birth, if you're not breastfeeding (Johnson, 2025)
- Much later, if you are (sometimes not for months!)

Your first few periods can:

- Be super heavy, weirdly light, or totally irregular
- Be accompanied by stronger cramps than usual
- Feel absolutely unfair

Other hormonal curveballs:

- **Discharge and odor changes:** Your vagina is doing her best, so be gentle
- **Body hair shifts:** Some falls out, some shows up in new places
- **Skin changes:** Hello, acne from your teen years

When to call your doctor:

- Foul-smelling discharge
- Bleeding that starts suddenly, heavy again after tapering off

- Intense itching, discomfort, or anything that just feels "off"

Remember, your body is still healing, and you are still learning. Give yourself grace to understand your new self not just physically, but emotionally, spiritually, and every way in between. You don't have to love every change. But you can honor them as part of the story you're writing: one that begins, again, with you.

YOUR BODY HAS BEEN through the storm and is learning to calm down. You're healing, growing, and redefining love. Now... let's talk about your baby. Chapter 7 is all about feeding and soothing the tiny human who just changed everything.

# 7

# THE BABY BUBBLE, FULL OF MILK AND MAGIC

I n these early weeks, day and night trade places. You'll wake up unsure what planet you're on, then cry because your baby yawned so beautifully. Welcome to the baby bubble!

Your living room may look like a bottle graveyard. Your phone search history will include things like, "Is green poop normal?" and "Will I ever sleep again?" And somewhere between feeding marathons and Googling "how to hold a baby without breaking them," you'll have a moment of quiet awe: *I made this tiny human.*

This chapter is for those first hazy weeks, when your shirt is always damp, your emotions are always right at the surface, and everything smells like milk and magic (and possibly throw-up). Let's talk about the feeding, the crying, the tiny fingernails that somehow make you weep. This is the messy, miraculous beginning, and you're doing better than you think.

## Your Baby's First Days

The first two weeks with a newborn are like moving to a new country where you don't speak the language, the clocks are broken, and everyone cries a lot, especially around 2 a.m.

You might expect to feel an instant, glowing connection with your baby, but maybe instead you feel tired and completely overwhelmed. That's okay. These early days aren't about perfect bonding. They're about survival, small wins, and falling in love in slow motion.

### What Those First 14 Days Really Look Like

Those first two weeks can feel like both a blur and a lifetime, each day shaped by tiny wins, big feelings, and the wild, beautiful mess of learning your baby (and yourself). Here's what to expect:

- **Day 1:** Your baby may be alert for the first hour or two after birth, then conk out like they've just pulled an all-nighter (because they have). You'll stare at their tiny face in disbelief. You might cry. Or feel nothing at all. Every reaction is normal.

- **Days 2–3:** Welcome to cluster feeding, swollen boobs, and hormone crashes. Your baby might feed all day and all night, which is their way of helping your milk come in. If you're breastfeeding, you will likely feed every two hours. Bottle-fed babies can usually go three to four hours between feeds. You might cry more now, and not just because of the hormones. Your body is sore, your brain is foggy, and the emotional rollercoaster has no seatbelt. It's okay to say, "I don't know what I'm doing."

- **Days 4–7:** Your baby might start waking up more between feeds, and by "waking up," we mean fussing, rooting, grunting, and using your chest as a mattress. The world is overstimulating for them, and it might be for you, too. Keep the lights soft, limit visitors if you want to, and take more photos than you think you'll want later. (You'll want them.)

- **Days 8–14:** You might finally catch a rhythm, or you might feel like it's all falling apart. Some parents start feeling emotionally connected to their baby around now. Others still feel detached, and that's also normal. Bonding isn't a deadline; it's a relationship. Give it time.

You'll also start to see your baby's patterns, cues, and unique quirks. You might even manage to shower twice this week. Victory!

### *Hormones, Hallucinations, and Phantom Baby Cries*

Around Day 3, many moms hit a wall emotionally, physically, and hormonally. Your milk is coming in, your estrogen is crashing, and you might even feel like you're falling apart. This is the "baby blues," and it happens to about 80% of new moms (*Baby Blues vs. Postpartum Depression*, 2019). You might question whether you're cut out for this.

You might start hearing your baby cry when they're not. You'll be in the shower and swear you hear them wailing. This is called phantom crying, and yes, it's a real thing. Your brain is rewiring itself to respond to every squeak, squawk, and sigh. Combine that with exhaustion, and it can feel like a hallucination, but you're not going crazy.

You might also:

- Wake up in panic because you dreamed the baby wasn't breathing
- Forget what day it is, or whether you brushed your teeth
- Stare at the fridge and have no clue what you came for

This is all part of the fog. Be gentle with yourself. Set alarms on your phone for meds, meals, hydration, and check-ins with yourself. Tape reminders to your fridge like "You're doing better than you think," or "Yes, eat something."

### Wait... Did I Eat Today?

Between endless feeds, diaper blowouts, and zombie-level fatigue, it's very easy to forget to eat, until you're dizzy, cranky, or crying over a granola bar.

Now is not the time to diet. Nourishing your body helps with milk supply, hormone balance, wound healing, and mental clarity (or at least prevents total collapse). Plus, eating is a tangible way to care for yourself while you care for your baby.

Here are some go-to favorites moms swear by:

- Freezer meals you can heat one-handed
- Crockpot soups you can eat while babywearing
- Protein shakes with a straw stuck in a diaper caddy
- Watermelon bowls (hydrating and easy to snack on)
- Cinnamon rolls at 2 a.m. because who's judging?

If you don't feel like eating, start small: trail mix, yogurt, apple slices, peanut butter toast. Think easy, not perfect.

I ate a rotisserie chicken over the sink while nursing. No regrets, I became a big foodie during this time period.

### The Feeding Frontlines

Whether you're nursing, pumping, combo-feeding, or formula-feeding, one thing is true: Feeding a newborn is not as simple as "insert milk, get sleep." It's a round-the-clock mission full of cracked nipples, bottle parts, and endless Googling. Let's make it less overwhelming, and remind you that how you feed your baby does not define your worth as a parent. Your child will eventually lick some kind of shopping cart, regardless of how you feed them as a newborn.

### Breastfeeding Basics

So, you decided to breastfeed, and you thought it would be "natural," right? Surprise! It's a learned dance, not an automatic reflex. And both of you are brand new at it.

Latching on can take practice. Try different positions: cradle hold, football hold, or side-lying (perfect for 3 a.m.). Your baby's mouth should cover most of the areola, not just the nipple. If it feels like a tiny piranha is attached to your boob, unlatch and try again, gently breaking the suction with a finger.

Nipple care is its own mini-career. Lanolin cream, cooling gel pads, and breast milk itself is liquid gold in more ways than one. Walk around topless if you want. You've earned the right.

How do you know baby's getting enough?

- At least six wet diapers a day after the first week
- Steady weight gain (your pediatrician will track this)
- Satisfied baby who unlatches and looks milk-drunk

Remember, most new moms struggle with breastfeeding. There's no shame in needing help. Lactation consultants are magical unicorns. If you can, find one early to save your nipples and frustration.

You don't have to dive into pumping milk immediately unless the baby is in the NICU or you're planning to combo feed (nursing and bottle). But if you do:

- Start with a low suction to avoid turning your nipples into raisins.

- Keep a snack and water bottle nearby. You'll be parched and starving.
- Don't compare your output to the social media mom with 40 ounces stored. Everyone's supply looks different.

Feeding your baby is not a test you pass or fail. It's a relationship you build, one feed at a time.

### Bottle Feeding and Formula Without Shame

There is nothing wrong with choosing to formula feed. Whether it's your first plan, your backup plan, or your mental health life-line, "fed is best" isn't just a slogan; it's a survival truth.

Here are a few tips to look out for in choosing bottles and formula:

- Look for BPA-free bottles with slow-flow nipples for newborns.
- Choose gentle formulas if your baby seems extra gassy or fussy (your pediatrician can help guide you).
- Premixed formulas are great for late-night feeds. They are pricey but clutch when you're delirious.

Combo-feeding is more common than people think. Some babies switch between breast and bottle like champs. Others need a little time to adjust. Either way, it's okay. There's no "one way" to feed a baby.

So let's debunk a few formula myths:

- **It causes constipation.** Only if it's not the right formula for your baby. Talk to your doctor.
- **You'll bond less.** This is absolutely false. Bonding happens through eye contact, soothing voices, cuddles, and care, not nipple type.

- **It's less natural.** So are air fryers and epidurals. That doesn't mean they're not lifesavers.

Here are a few tips to help you with bottle-prep basics:

- Use the scoop that comes with the formula.
- Warm bottles in a mug of hot water or a bottle warmer, never a microwave.
- Store mixed formula in the fridge for up to 24 hours unless the instructions say otherwise.

There is no award for suffering through a feeding method that breaks you. Feed the baby. Protect the mom.

### Feeding After the Fog

Once the adrenaline wears off and sleep deprivation kicks in, night feeds can feel like you're trapped in a midnight sitcom you didn't audition for. Here are a few tools to make this nightmare easier:

- A feeding caddy with water, snacks, nipple cream, burp cloths, and a phone charger
- A partner who brings the baby to you (and rubs your feet if they're extra)
- A soft night light so you don't blind yourself at 2 a.m.

It's also important to understand when your baby is really hungry, or when they're just crabby or want some cuddling. Here are a few hunger cues to look out for:

- Rooting (baby turns their head like a tiny search engine)
- Hand-sucking or smacking lips
- Crying is usually a last resort

If the thought of feeding makes your skin crawl, or you're constantly crying, you're not alone, and you deserve support. Talk to your doctor or therapist. You're not weak. You're running a marathon on an empty tank.

**The Sleep S.O.S.**

Sleep in the newborn days is not a schedule but a wild experiment in human endurance. Just when you drift off, a tiny alarm clock with flailing arms reminds you that your body no longer belongs to you. Let's figure out how to survive the sleep saga.

*Understanding Newborn Sleep (And Lack Thereof)*

If you're asking, "When will my baby sleep through the night?" the short answer is: Not yet. And no, you didn't do anything wrong.

Newborn sleep cycles are short, usually 20–50 minutes (*Typical Sleep Behaviour...*, n.d.). They spend more time in light sleep, which means they twitch, grunt, and startle often. This is normal. Their little brains are still sorting out day from night, and hunger from habit.

Safe sleep recommendations say babies should sleep (Ben-Joseph, 2022):

- On their back
- In a flat, firm bassinet or crib (no pillows or loose blankets)
- Room temp: 68–72 °F (20–22 °C)
- Use a sleep sack or swaddle (arms in for newborns, out when they start rolling)
- In the room with you for at least six months
- Add white noise to mimic the womb

But let's be honest: Contact naps, accidental co-sleeping, and dozing with a baby on your chest happen. We're not here to judge. We're here to inform and keep things safe without shame.

You don't have to be productive while your baby sleeps. You are allowed to sleep, too. Or just stare at a wall in silence. That counts.

**Tips to Survive on Little to No Sleep**

- Tag-team nights if you have a partner.
- Keep quick snacks and water within arm's reach.
- Use a white noise machine for everyone.
- Nap when you can; even 20 minutes helps.
- Remind yourself that you're not lazy or crazy; you're adjusting to a new human's rhythm.

*Where Sleep Actually Happens*

You can read 100 baby sleep books, or you can realize that your baby is going to fall asleep wherever they feel safe, warm, and loved. Also, there's just no point in trying to get your baby to sleep when you've misread the cues of having a cramp for being tired. Here are a few tips to spot sleepy cues:

- Yawning
- Rubbing eyes
- Turning away from stimulation
- The weird "I'm tired but wired" burst of energy

"Don't spoil a baby by soothing them to sleep." I'm sure you've heard that line many times before. But let me assure you that you just can't spoil a newborn baby. Our world is a scary, cold place for them, and they need their mama's love. A few soothing tricks to try:

- Rocking or swaying
- Shushing sounds (even a vacuum app!)
- Pacifier (if baby takes one)
- A song you hum so much you dream it

Eventually, you'll get it right. You'll realize that you understand your baby's needs, and after a few weeks (or months), they might even sleep through the night. Once that happens, ask yourself: *What moment made me feel like I was finally getting the hang of this?*

It could be a burp you caught before a spit-up. A 90-minute nap. Or the first time you made your baby laugh. Hold onto that moment. It means more than you know.

OKAY, you've tracked milestones, powered through shots and side effects, and memorized the color of poop like it's your job. But now what? What happens after the baby calendar says "Week 12"?

The next chapter is your bridge from surviving the fourth trimester to thriving in what comes next.

# 8

# FINDING YOURSELF WHILE RAISING SOMEONE ELSE

You stand in the hallway, the baby finally asleep, and catch your reflection in the mirror; your hair is a mess, your eyes are tired, and your heart has cracked open in a way you didn't expect. When will you feel like yourself again?

Maybe the answer isn't *going back*. Maybe it's *becoming*.

Because you're not just raising a child. You're also becoming a new version of you. One who knows what exhaustion tastes like but also how deeply you can love. One who sometimes misses your old life and still wouldn't trade this one.

As Brené Brown said, "Who we are is how we lead, especially in motherhood" (Brown, 2018). And leading, in this new season, starts with honoring both your baby and yourself.

This chapter is for the in-between stretch: the days when your baby starts noticing the world and you start noticing yourself again. Not who you were before, but who you're becoming now.

.  .  .

## THE NEXT STRETCH

The newborn fog is beginning to lift. You're blinking into the daylight of a new phase: less fragile, more interactive, and sometimes more exhausting in new ways. The baby who once curled like a comma on your chest is now wide-eyed, wiggly, and ready to discover the world.

You're discovering things, too, like how much more you've learned than you realized, how your instincts are louder now, and how pieces of your old self are meeting the new one. This next stretch is about growth, your baby's and yours.

### Understanding Months 3–4

At around three months, your baby becomes noticeably more social. Smiles start coming faster and more intentionally. You might even hear your first giggle, which has the power to make your sleep-deprived heart melt. They'll start tracking your face when you move, following objects with their eyes, and reaching for toys (or your hair). These aren't just cute milestones. They're signs of huge brain development.

Feeding may start to settle into a more manageable rhythm, with longer stretches between sessions and more efficient nursing or bottle sessions. You might even get lucky with a longer nighttime sleep window. But don't be surprised if sleep suddenly falls apart again: hello, sleep regressions! It's not that you're doing anything wrong; it's that your baby's brain is in overdrive, practicing all these new skills, even in their sleep.

Here's the emotional twist: Your baby is more awake, more alert, and more demanding of your energy. You might feel like you have to be "on" all the time now, performing a gentle dance of stimulation, soothing, and snacks. This shift can feel both energizing and exhausting. You're stepping into a new phase, one that requires a different kind of presence. You're not just feeding and swaddling anymore. You're relating.

**Journal Prompt**

What did I notice about my baby's personality this month?

*Big Shifts in Months 5–6*

By the time your baby hits five or six months, everything starts moving faster: rolling, scooting, toe-grabbing, and early attempts to launch themselves off the play mat like a tiny gymnast. Mobility changes the game. Your once-stationary baby now wants to explore, and your arms are suddenly very tired.

This is also when many babies begin showing signs of readiness for solids, watching you eat with fascination, trying to grab your food, or sitting up with support. Introducing solids is messy and hilarious, but it's also a moment that makes many parents emotional. *How did we go from cluster feeding to pureed carrots so fast?*

Play takes on new meaning now, too. Mirrors, soft books, and textured toys are all invitations to curiosity. You'll start to see patterns emerge in your baby's preferences and personality. Some love tickles, others just want to stare at ceiling fans like they're hosting a TED Talk.

At the same time, something strange may start happening inside you. You may find yourself missing pieces of the person you were before. Not because you don't love your baby, but because you're starting to come up for air. You might want to see friends again or just sit somewhere without being touched. These desires don't mean you're ungrateful. They mean you're human.

I bought a fancy sensory toy, but my son prefers the crinkly wipes package. Should've just saved the $30 and handed him trash. It was a reminder that babies will play with anything.

### Creating Rhythms, Not Routines

You might start feeling the pressure now, whether from parenting blogs, family advice, or your internal voice, to get your baby on a "schedule." But here's the truth: You don't need a rigid routine. What you need are rhythms. Gentle patterns that give your day some predictability without the stress of minute-by-minute planning.

A typical rhythm might look like wake, feed, play, nap, repeat. But how that plays out will change weekly, sometimes daily. Maybe your baby naps like a dream for three days, then decides sleep is a betrayal. That doesn't mean you've failed. It means they're growing.

If you're craving some structure, try a flexible rhythm chart that leaves room for change. Time blocks, like a morning rest window or some late-afternoon play, can help ground you without boxing you in. Rhythms help babies feel safe and secure, and they help you feel just a bit more like you know what planet you're on.

And remember: There's no gold star for following a TikTok-perfect schedule. There's only your peace and sanity.

I followed a nap schedule today. It lasted exactly one nap. We're back to chaos and vibes.

### The "New Normal:" Life Logistics Post-Baby

Your body has healed (mostly), your baby is growing (rapidly), and somehow, people expect you to "bounce back" like the last few months weren't the emotional equivalent of a tornado in a diaper. Welcome to the "new normal," a place where you're trying to redis-cover your rhythms, your identity, and your tolerance for laundry.

It's not just about bottles and burp cloths anymore. It's about work and relationships, as well. This stretch brings big decisions and even bigger feelings. And while it may look different for every family, one truth stands: You're not alone in figuring it out.

*Back to Work, or Not*

Returning to work (or deciding not to) is one of the most personal, emotional, and logistically tangled decisions of early parenthood. It's not just a financial calculation. It's a heart-level negotiation. Maybe you're craving adult conversation and the thrill of wearing a clean shirt. Perhaps you're sobbing at the idea of leaving your baby for even an hour. Both can be true at once.

You might find yourself crunching numbers, scanning daycare waitlists, and Googling "how to pump in a storage closet without crying." If you're hiring a nanny or leaning on family help, there's a whole new dynamic to navigate: trust, schedules, and the weirdness of someone else learning your baby's quirks. Let's look at a few gentle ways to ease the transition:

- Start with short practice runs. Leave your baby with their caregiver while you take a walk or run errands.
- Introduce new faces slowly and stay calm during handoffs. Your baby picks up on your energy.
- With daycare, visit the space ahead of time, talk to teachers, and label everything.
- If you're hiring a nanny, do a working interview where you stay nearby, so both you and the nanny can get comfortable.
- If family is helping, have kind-but-clear conversations about routines, boundaries, and expectations.

Then there's the emotional toll: the guilt, the brain fog, the fear of being "too much mom" at home or "not enough mom" at work. It's real. You're not doing it wrong. You're just trying to live two lives in one body.

This isn't about choosing between a career and motherhood. It's about reshaping what work means to you now.

The first day back at work, I cried the entire drive and then sat in the parking lot practicing how to smile. I love my job. I also missed my baby so much it hurt.

### Intimacy, Body, and the Bedroom

Let's just say it: Postpartum intimacy can be weird. Your body feels like it belongs to someone else, because it kind of did for the past nine months, and suddenly you're expected to feel sexy when you're still wearing nursing pads.

For some, libido returns quickly. For others, it takes months. Many experience pain, dryness, or discomfort long after the six-week "green light" from their doctor. Emotionally, you might feel miles away from intimacy, even with a loving partner. Or you might crave closeness but not know how to get there.

Start small. Connection isn't only about sex. It's about eye contact, quiet moments, and a hand on your back while you brush your teeth. Let affection rebuild slowly. Communicate honestly. Above all, ditch the myth that you "should be ready by now." Readiness isn't about a date on the calendar. It's about comfort, trust, and healing.

If you're experiencing pain or pelvic floor issues, know that help exists. A pelvic floor therapist can offer gentle, practical guidance for healing, not just physically, but emotionally, too.

I thought once I got the go-ahead, sex would be back to normal. It wasn't. I had to relearn how to be in my body again, not just next to my baby.

### You're Not in This Alone: Partner Power

This chapter isn't complete without talking about the other player on your team. Whether you're married, partnered, co-parenting, or navigating it solo with support, your connection to your village (and especially your partner, if you have one) matters more than ever.

Postpartum can make even the strongest relationships wobble. You're sleep-deprived, touched out, and suddenly managing an entire new human and all their needs. The invisible labor alone (who's ordering diapers, scheduling appointments, remembering which boob was last?) can breed resentment fast.

That's why communication is everything. Not polished conversations but real ones. "Can you take the baby while I shower?" counts. So does "I'm overwhelmed and I need a break without being asked to explain it." Avoid falling into the micromanaging trap. Instead, share the mental load. Partners don't have to "help." They have to parent.

Create small rituals that bring you back to each other: trading off baby duty at night, sending each other funny memes, or sitting together for 10 quiet minutes after bedtime.

And don't forget to let them read *You Will Rock as a Dad!* (link it, buy it, or tape it to the fridge). Because this is a two-player game. You were never meant to carry it all.

YOU DID IT. You faced the fog, found your rhythm, lost yourself a little, and started to come back home to you. No, it wasn't perfect, but you kept showing up, one diaper, one meltdown, and one midnight laugh at a time.

This isn't the end of your story; it's the part where you realize you were never "just" becoming a mom. You were becoming more.

Let's celebrate how far you've come and what's still waiting for you.

# CONCLUSION

Remember when you didn't even know what trimester you were in? When you were Googling acronyms and symptoms, and wondering how on earth you'd ever feel ready? That version of you couldn't possibly have imagined the woman reading this now.

You've weathered contractions, cluster feeds, hormonal avalanches, and identity earthquakes. You've met the baby, and the new you, in stages. You've cried in the shower, laughed at phantom cries, fed a small human in the dark, and learned to function on hope, snacks, and sheer grit.

You haven't just survived. You've transformed.

This is a mirror, and what it reflects is someone learning to lead with love, even when she doesn't have all the answers. Someone who's growing, not in spite of the chaos, but through it.

You were never broken. You were becoming. And you'll continue to become as you weather the storm of caring for your baby through the first year and surviving the wonderful terror that is toddlerhood.

Motherhood remakes you. It strips away what doesn't matter, sharpens what does, and invites you to love more fiercely, both your baby and yourself. There is no perfect version of this. There is only the real, raw, and remarkable version you are living.

So pause. Breathe. Let yourself feel proud for making it through the hardest parts, and for showing up with heart.

This is not the end. It's just the part where the story opens up wider. You've got this, and you're not alone.

Welcome to the rest of your becoming. And remember, *You Will Rock as a Mom!*

Your friend,

Sierra

# BIBLIOGRAPHY

*Baby blues vs. postpartum depression.* (2019). South Dakota Department of Health. https://doh.sd.gov/topics/mch/womens-health/postpartum-health/care-after-delivery/postpartum-depression/

Ben-Joseph, E. P. (2022, July). *Sleep and your newborn (for parents).* Nemours Kids Health. https://kidshealth.org/en/parents/sleepnewborn.html

Blanding, T. (2024, August 26). *36 weeks pregnant.* BabyCenter. https://www.babycenter.com/pregnancy/week-by-week/36-weeks-pregnant

Boyd-Barrett, C. (2023, September 28). Glucose screening and glucose tolerance tests. *BabyCenter.* https://www.babycenter.com/pregnancy/health-and-safety/glucose-screening-and-glucose-tolerance-tests_1483

Brown, B. (2018). *Dare to lead.* Random House.

Burch, K. (2024, August 27). *39 weeks pregnant.* BabyCenter. https://www.babycenter.com/pregnancy/week-by-week/39-weeks-pregnant

*Caffeine.* (2022, September 1). MotherToBaby. https://mothertobaby.org/fact-sheets/caffeine-pregnancy/

*Children's Health Insurance Program (CHIP).* (2022). Medicaid. https://www.medicaid.gov/chip

Curran, K. (2021, May 27). *Moms feel unprepared for and unsupported during postpartum.* Lansinoh. https://lansinoh.com/blogs/birth-prep-recovery/moms-feel-unprepared-for-and-unsupported-during-postpartum?srsltid=AfmBOopPoG6MuNPPeYBcfxAUpWmYpdofuFkfzy-qjCQIaEL7xJm5syon

De Pietro, M. (2023, October 9). *Lightning crotch: What to know about shooting pain during pregnancy.* Medical News Today. https://www.medicalnewstoday.com/articles/322088

Deganich, M., Boudreaux C., & Benmerzouga, I. (2022). Toxoplasmosis infection during pregnancy. *Tropical Medicine and Infectious Disease, 8*(1), 3. https://doi.org/10.3390/tropicalmed8010003

Dekker, R. (2017, September 13). *The evidence on: due dates.* Evidence-Based First-trimester Birth. https://evidencebasedbirth.com/evidence-on-due-dates/

Donaldson-Evans, C. (2024, September 3). *Week 9 of pregnancy.* What to Expect. https://www.whattoexpect.com/pregnancy/week-by-week/week-9.aspx

Donaldson-Evans, C. (2025a, January 9). *What are Braxton Hicks contractions and are they the same as false labor?* What to Expect. https://www.whattoexpect.com/pregnancy/symptoms-and-solutions/braxton-hicks-contractions.aspx

Donaldson-Evans, C. (2025b, January 17). *16 signs of labor — Here's what to expect when it's go-time.* What to Expect. https://www.whattoexpect.com/pregnancy/labor-signs

*Family and Medical Leave Act.* (n.d.). U.S. Department of Labor. https://www.dol.gov/agencies/whd/fmla

*First-trimester screening, nuchal translucency and NIPT.* (2022, December 28). John Hopkins Medicine. https://www.hopkinsmedicine.org/health/treatment-tests-and-therapies/first-trimester-screening-nuchal-translucency-and-nipt

Gates, M. (2024a, August 20). 6 weeks pregnant. *BabyCenter.* https://www.babycenter.com/pregnancy/week-by-week/6-weeks-pregnant

Gates, M. (2024b, August 21). 8 weeks pregnant. *BabyCenter.* https://www.babycenter.com/pregnancy/week-by-week/8-weeks-pregnant

Gates, M. (2025, May 30). *7 weeks pregnant.* BabyCenter. https://www.babycenter.com/pregnancy/week-by-week/7-weeks-pregnant

Guardian Editorial Team. (2016). *Short-term disability insurance for maternity and pregnancy leave.* Guardian. https://www.guardianlife.com/disability-insurance/pregnancy

Hartshorn, J. (2025, May 14). *The ultimate checklist of baby must-haves (and don't-needs) for your registry.* Parents. https://www.parents.com/baby/gear/registries-buying-guides/baby-shopping-guide/

Holland, K. (2024, November 25). *Early pregnancy symptoms.* Healthline. https://www.healthline.com/health/pregnancy/early-symptoms-timeline

*How to take time for self-care with kids in the room.* (2025, May 20). Scary Mommy. https://www.scarymommy.com/parenting/you-dont-have-to-be-alone-to-take-time-for-self-care

Ingram, A. (2025, March 19). *What to do when your baby bites while breastfeeding.* Swaddles 'N Bottles. https://www.swaddlesnbottles.com/what-to-do-when-your-baby-bites-while-breastfeeding/

Jabaz, D. & Abed, M. (2023, November 12). *Sonography 2nd trimester assessment, protocols, and interpretation.* PubMed; StatPearls Publishing. https://www.ncbi.nlm.nih.gov/books/NBK570574/

Jennifer Kelly Geddes. (2022, November 28). *Your guide to pregnancy hormones.* What to Expect. https://www.whattoexpect.com/pregnancy/pregnancy-health/pregnancy-hormones.aspx

Jenny. (2015, September 3). *Surprising things you can eat in pregnancy!* Midwife and Life. https://midwifeandlife.com/what-you-can-and-cant-eat-in-pregnancy-a-guide/

Jenny. (2018, December 5). *What to expect at your pregnancy booking in appointment with the midwife (UK) and questions to ask.* Midwife and Life. https://midwifeandlife.com/what-to-expect-at-your-pregnancy-booking-in-appointment-with-the-midwife-uk-questions-to-ask/

Jenny. (2021, July 30). *What to do while on maternity leave.* Midwife and Life. https://midwifeandlife.com/what-to-do-while-on-maternity-leave/

Jenny. (2023, January 30). *11 things to do when you find out you're pregnant.* Midwife and Life. https://midwifeandlife.com/11-things-to-do-when-you-find-out-youre-pregnant/

Jenny. (2024, September 27). *Natural ways to alleviate morning sickness: Safe remedies for expecting mothers.* Midwife and Life. https://midwifeandlife.com/natural-ways-to-alleviate-morning-sickness-safe-remedies-for-expecting-mothers/

Johnson, T. C. (2025, April 19). *First period after pregnancy: What to expect.* WebMD. https://www.webmd.com/baby/first-period-after-pregnancy-what-to-expect

Longman, H. (2024, November 26). *How much does a baby cost per month?* BabyCenter. https://www.babycenter.com/family/money/top-baby-costs

Marple, K. (2024, August 20). 5 weeks pregnant. *BabyCenter.* https://www.babycenter.com/pregnancy/week-by-week/5-weeks-pregnant

Marple, K. (2025, May 30). *10 weeks pregnant.* BabyCenter. https://www.babycenter.com/pregnancy/week-by-week/10-weeks-pregnant

Miles, K. (2022). *How to get relief from round ligament pain.* BabyCenter. https://www.babycenter.com/pregnancy/health-and-safety/round-ligament-pain_205

Morrison, A. (2017, July 20). *12 weeks pregnant.* Pregnant Chicken. https://pregnantchicken.com/pregnancy-calendar-week-12/

Morrison, A. (2018, January 20). *6 weeks pregnant.* Pregnant Chicken. https://pregnantchicken.com/pregnancy-calendar-week-6/

Nordqvist, J. (2023, November 10). *Miscarriage: Warning signs, treatments, and prevention.* Medical News Today. https://www.medicalnewstoday.com/articles/262941

*Nutrition during pregnancy.* (2022). The American College of Obstetricians and Gynecologists. https://www.acog.org/womens-health/faqs/nutrition-during-pregnancy

O'Connor, A. (2022, October 14). *Linea nigra.* What to Expect. https://www.whattoexpect.com/pregnancy/symptoms-and-solutions/linea-nigra.aspx

Patwal, S. (2025, March 5). *26 foods to avoid during pregnancy.* MomJunction. https://www.momjunction.com/articles/foods-definitely-avoid-pregnancy_0022296/

Peterson, G. (2023, May 2). *When does a fetus have a heartbeat?* Human Life International. https://www.hli.org/resources/when-does-a-fetus-have-a-heartbeat/

Pickett, K. (2024, February 29). *The first-time mom's guide to thriving, not just surviving.* MilkDust for Moms. https://milkdust.com/blogs/health/the-first-time-moms-guide-to-thriving-not-just-surviving?srsltid=AfmBOoo-_0_zEi84Xpvzh5AbXKvzQIfsFMSB6hZ-CSN1Ya_QscyQQtUS

Pillai, S. (2025, February 17). *10 exercises to avoid during pregnancy.* MomJunction. https://www.momjunction.com/articles/exercises-you-should-avoid-during-pregnancy_00122653/

*Policy basics: Special supplemental nutrition program for women, infants, and children.* (2022, October 5). Center on Budget and Policy Priorities. https://www.cbpp.org/research/food-assistance/special-supplemental-nutrition-program-for-women-infants-and-children

Raines, D. A. & Cooper, D. B. (2023, August 8). *Braxton Hicks contractions.* Nih.gov; StatPearls Publishing. https://www.ncbi.nlm.nih.gov/books/NBK470546/

*Routine tests during pregnancy.* (2021, July). American College of Obstetricians and Gynecologists. https://www.acog.org/womens-health/faqs/routine-tests-during-pregnancy

Schmitt, M. (2021, January 11). *Beyond "near me": How to find the best OB-GYN for you.* HealthPartners. https://www.healthpartners.com/blog/tips-for-finding-the-right-ob-gyn/

*Screening for group B strep bacteria.* (2025, May 1). Centers for Disease Control and Prevention. https://www.cdc.gov/group-b-strep/testing/index.html

Simelela, N. (2024). *The unacceptable stigma and shame women face after baby loss must end.* World Health Organization. https://www.who.int/news-room/spotlight/why-we-need-to-talk-about-losing-a-baby/unacceptable-stigma-and-shame

Smith, J. A., Fox, K. A. & Clark, S. M. (2025, March 31). *Patient education: Nausea and vomiting of pregnancy (Beyond the basics).* Up to Date. https://www.uptodate.com/contents/nausea-and-vomiting-of-pregnancy-beyond-the-basics/print

*Supplemental nutrition assistance program (SNAP).* (2025, February 20). Food and Nutrition Service. https://www.fns.usda.gov/snap/supplemental-nutrition-assistance-program

*Typical sleep behaviour (1) – newborns 0 to 3 months.* (n.d.). Better Health. https://www.betterhealth.vic.gov.au/health/healthyliving/typical-sleep-behaviour-nb-0-3-months

Uscher, J. (2024, November 2). *Anemia in pregnancy.* WebMD. https://www.webmd.com/baby/anemia-in-pregnancy

Wahlberg, R. (2025, May 6). *Tiny seed to giant watermelon: How big your baby is this week.* BabyCenter. https://www.babycenter.com/pregnancy/your-body/how-big-is-my-baby-week-by-week-fruit-and-veggie-comparisons_5223185

Ward, E. M. (2006, May 31). *Coping with pregnancy food cravings.* WebMD. https://www.webmd.com/baby/features/coping-with-pregnancy-food-cravings

*WIC: USDA's special supplemental nutrition program for women, infants, and children.* (2023). Food and Nutrition Services. https://www.fns.usda.gov/wic

Winston, R. & Chicot, R. (2016). The importance of early bonding on the long-term mental health and resilience of children. *London Journal of Primary Care, 8*(1), 12–14. https://doi.org/10.1080/17571472.2015.1133012

www.ingramcontent.com/pod-product-compliance
Lightning Source LLC
Chambersburg PA
CBHW051317120626
46547CB00015B/2271